A Friendly Guide to
The Book of Psalms

Mary Reaburn nds

Published in Australia by
Garratt Publishing
32 Glenvale Crescent
Mulgrave, VIC 3170
www.garrattpublishing.com.au

Text copyright © 2022 Mary Reaburn NDS
All rights reserved. Except as provided by the Australian copyright law, no part of this book may be reproduced in any way without permission in writing from the publisher.

Design, typesetting and calligraphy by Lynne Muir
Images copyright © p 33 photo by Jane Austin, Statue in St Francis Church central Melbourne, artist Pauline Clayton; Wikipedia: pp1, 6, 15, 16, 19, 22, 28, 30, 34, 41, 46, 52; iStock: Cover, pp 1, 3–5, 7–15, 17–22, 24–27, 29, 32, 34, 35, 3–40, 42– 45, 47–49, 50, 51, 53– 56.

Scripture quotations are drawn from the New Revised Standard Version of the Bible, copyright © 1989 by the Division of Christian Education of the National Council of the Churches of Christ in the USA.

Used by permission.
All rights reserved.

Nihil Obstat: Reverend Monsignor Peter J Kenny STD, Diocesan Censor, Catholic Archdiocese of Melbourne
Imprimatur: Very Reverend Joseph Caddy, AM, Lic. Soc. Sci VG, Vicar General, Catholic Archdiocese of Melbourne
Date: 30 September 2021
The Nihil Obstat and Imprimatur are official declarations that a book or pamphlet is free of doctrinal or moral error. No implication is contained therein that those who have granted the Nihil Obstat and Imprimatur agree with the contents, opinions or statements expressed. They do not necessarily signify that the work is approved as a basic text for catechetical instruction.

ISBN 9781922484246

Cataloguing in Publication information for this title is available from the National Library of Australia.
www.nla.gov.au

The author and publisher gratefully acknowledge the permission granted to reproduce the copyright material in this book. Every effort has been made to trace copyright holders and to obtain their permission for the use of copyright material.

The publisher apologises for any errors or omissions in the above list and would be grateful if notified of any corrections that should be incorporated in future reprints or editions of this book.

DEDICATION

This book is dedicated to the scholarship and memory of Angelo O'Hagan OFM (1929–2016). My teacher.

CONTENTS

INTRODUCTION 3

AN INVITATION INTO THE
BOOK OF PSALMS 6

PSALMS AND LIFE — THEN AND NOW 9

GENRES IN PSALMS 14

THE BOOKS OF THE PSALTER 20

MEET GOD THROUGH IMAGERY 24

KING DAVID — THE PATRON
OF THE PSALMS 29

JESUS PRAYED THE PSALMS 33

HEBREW POETRY 38

COMMUNITY PRAYER 44

TEMPLE WORSHIP 51

CONCLUSION: SPEAKING
TO THE BELOVED 53

GLOSSARY 54

FURTHER READING 55

Cover: Tree of Life, artist unknown
Title page: Alleluya by Thomas Cooper Gotch circa 1896

Introduction

Pope Francis has called the Church to a deeper immersion into the Scriptures. He has named the third Sunday of the year as a 'Sunday of the Word of God'. In Australia, the Catholic bishops have chosen to mark this on the first Sunday of February so as not to conflict with Australia Day. The Pope announced this on September 30th 2019, the feast of St Jerome, the patron saint of Scripture lovers.

The Scriptures will nourish us and sometimes challenge us if we spend time with them. They can be life-changing. In Luke 2:19 Mary contemplates the events she has experienced and I like to imagine her allowing the stories of her people, the Word of God, to shape how she came to understand her own experience. This process of meaning-making requires reflection on life and a familiarity with the Word of God in the Bible. Jesus, as an observant Jew, would have prayed the psalms personally and with his people, especially when celebrating the feasts in the Temple. The Evangelists witness to this in placing texts from the psalms on his lips as he dies. The Book of Psalms is the most frequently cited Old Testament book in the New Testament.

The psalms have a special place in both Jewish and Christian tradition and today, as in past centuries, they invite us into a life-long dialogue with God. The psalms are the most intimate communication of the individual and community with the Beloved. They help us speak truthfully about our experiences and feelings; they also invite us to be willing to wait for God's response. In that they are our words to God they can be raw and honest. In that they are God's word spoken to us they humble and exalt us as we listen attentively. In this they differ from most of the rest of the Bible. They are profound, enigmatic, enticing, sometimes repulsive and always so very honest.

Psalms are familiar and yet strange. I have been teaching the psalms for more than thirty years and yet they still surprise me and call me to listen more carefully to the revelation within them. Metaphors abound and are both familiar and unfamiliar. The tree and chaff of Psalm 1 are familiar but the bottle full of tears of Psalm 56 is far less so. We all know Psalm 23, *The Lord is my Shepherd*; yet we sometimes miss the other striking image in this Psalm, the banquet, the table the Lord prepares before me.

A Friendly Guide to the Book of Psalms aims to slow the reader down, so as to go deeply into the text and to be amazed at what is there. Often, psalms speak of encountering enemies and of vengeance and we might tend to shy away from them; but such

Numbering of the Psalms

You will notice that sometimes the same psalm is numbered differently in different contexts. This is because the system of numbering the psalms in the Greek tradition and the Hebrew tradition is slightly different. The Latin follows the Greek numbering and Catholics have followed the Latin. The Christian Orthodox communities follow the Greek numbering. The Reform communities follow the Hebrew numbering. In this *Friendly Guide* the Hebrew numbering is followed.

Psalms 1–9: same numbering in all traditions.
(Greek Pss 9 & 10 are one psalm)

Psalms 10–113: one difference in numbering. (Greek is one behind the Hebrew.)

Psalms 113–115 – Ps 113 Greek = Pss 114-115 in Hebrew
(Hebrew Ps 116 = Greek Pss 114 & 115)
Psalm 116 – 147 one difference in numbering.
(Hebrew Ps 147 = Greek Pss 146 & 147)
Psalms 148 – 150 same numbering in all traditions.

The text is the same but the way it is divided is different.

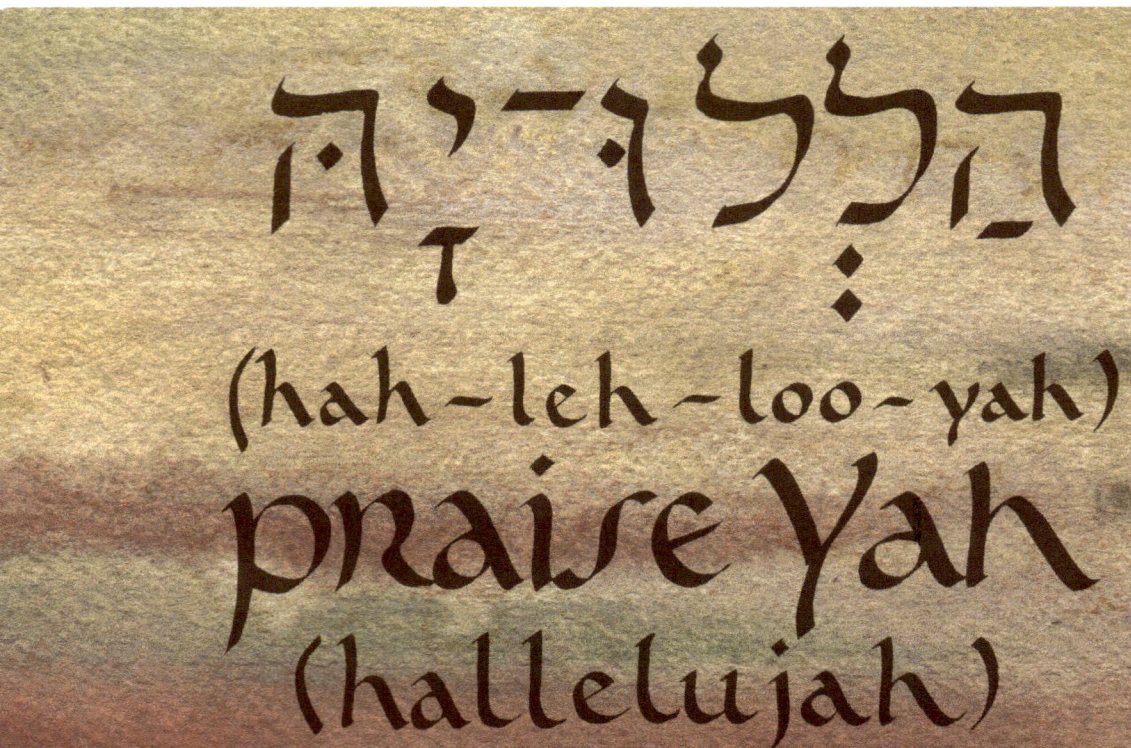

(hah-leh-loo-yah)
praise Yah
(hallelujah)

Halleluyah

This is a joy-filled command translated as 'Praise the LORD'. It is derived from two Hebrew words: הַלְלוּ (*hallelu*, masculine imperative meaning 'praise') and יָהּ, (*Yah* or *Jah*, an abbreviation of the special name of God YHWH). It is an exhortation to all to praise God. The NRSV does not use Alleluia or Halleluia or Ḥalleluyah, instead translating the word as 'Praise the LORD'. It is to be found in psalms: 104-106; 111-113; 115-117; 135; 146-150. It usually occurs at the beginning or end of the psalm. You will notice that all occurrences are in the final third of the Psalter, moving towards a crescendo of praise.

psalms invite us to plumb the depths of our own hearts with honesty and allow God to touch the pain and anger. The psalms also invite us to turn towards God in the experience of wonder, of gratitude, of a heightened sense of being the recipient of goodness. Particularly at times of deep emotion, the psalms offer us words with which to speak our truth to the Beloved.

Many encounter the psalms as the response in the Liturgy of the Word. Sadly, the psalm is seldom mentioned in homilies. Some pray the Prayer of the Church, (Divine Office, Liturgy of the Hours) which abounds with psalms. Priests are required to pray this daily and fortunately many others are now engaging this ancient practice of praying the Liturgy of the Hours so as to mark the turning points of the day with prayer.

The *Friendly Guide* offers a way to explore the ocean of emotions, metaphors, poetic succinctness and surprises behind the power of God's Word in the Book of Psalms. The psalms are like an ancient city that we explore and then excavate in order to understand their depth and story more fully. In order to excavate the psalms, you will need a bible beside you (preferably the NRSV translation): the text will reveal its secrets only when you attend to it with care.

Unfortunately, it is not possible to comment on all of the 150 psalms, so some representative texts will be explored. However, with these examples, the background information will help the reader reach a deeper understanding of their meaning, evoking an engagement with the text and a dialogue with their theology.

> The term 'Word of God' refers to the Bible. It also refers to Jesus who is the Word made flesh. In this book, it is used as a way of speaking of the Scriptures.

An Invitation into the Book of Psalms

> **Book of Psalms: the Psalter**
>
> Both terms refer to the collection of 150 psalms in the Bible. There are other psalms in the Bible which are not included in this collection: these are often called *canticles*. The most famous of the canticles is the *Magnificat*, the song placed on the lips of Mary by the evangelist Luke. In 1 Samuel 2 we find the prayer of Hannah, which seems to have influenced the Magnificat; it too is a psalm, even though not found in the Psalter. In the Book of Daniel we find the Canticle of the Three Young Men. The Book of Isaiah contains hymns and laments, which are characteristic of psalms. The word *psalm* is from the Greek translation and refers to songs accompanied by stringed instruments. The word used to name this book in Jewish tradition is *Tehillim*, praises. This word comes from the same root as *Halleluyah*. Thus, the Jewish tradition characterises this book as praise, even though there are more laments than songs of praise.

The Book of Psalms is one of the longest books in the Bible and it contains a variety of prayers, reflections and invitations. These are all in poetic form and are filled with images and sayings that inspire us and allow us to touch a range of emotions.

These ancient texts are remarkably current and tantalising. They ask questions about the meaning of life: *What are human beings that you keep them in mind?* (Ps 8:4); *Even before a word is on my tongue, O Lord, you know it completely.* (Ps 139:4); *How long, O LORD? Will you forget me forever?* (Ps 13:1)

The psalms sometimes ask the questions we cannot articulate or even dare to utter. Many of them are addressed to God and are therefore prayers. These prayers give us words when words may fail us; the psalms give us words to express our deepest emotions and concerns. Because psalms are also Scripture, they are, in a very real sense, God's Word. Thus, psalms are both our words to God and God's gift, God's Word, to us. They are a dialogue in themselves and they invite us into dialogue with God and with self and with community.

King David has long been associated with the psalms: he is known in the tradition as a musician and composer. We even read of him soothing King Saul with his playing (1 Sam 16:23). Many of the psalms have a heading that links a specific psalm to David, and some even specify an event in David's life to which the particular psalm refers. Yet most scholars today acknowledge that

Right: David composing the psalms with Melodia behind him, from the Paris Psalter, Byzantine, 10th century

David is not the composer of the majority of them. However, his name continues to evoke links with the psalms. His name provides authority.

Many psalms were chanted in Temple liturgy, and we see this communal context over and over. Most of the psalms were written to be chanted, sung to a simple melody. The Israelites knew, as we do today, that a chant stays with us longer in our hearts and minds than does a simple recitation. Even though the very religious context of the Temple was a springboard for the initial writing of psalms, they also reflect the experiences and emotions of daily life in biblical times.

PSALM 1

Daily life is at the heart of the psalmist's concerns from the start. Psalm 1 invites us into the Book of Psalms. It is both an invitation into the book and an invitation into life. First, it describes a happy person. *Happy is the one who ...* If I may use the Hebrew somewhat literally it says: *happy is the one who does not WALK with the counsel of the wicked or STAND with sinners or SIT with scoffers.* The only remaining thing is to lie down, asleep. In other words, the whole life of the happy person is not to be caught up with the journey of those who promote wickedness. The ways of God are represented by *Torah*, God's teaching. This teaching is the delight of the happy person who meditates on it day and night. Many who have prayed this psalm ask: but how can I meditate on God's teaching day and night; I need to work and to spend time with my family?

The answer is to be found in our living: our WALKING, STANDING and SITTING. When we go about the ordinariness of life we are invited to ponder God's ways. It is not all about studying the text, but living the text, seeing God and God's ways amidst the totality of life *because* we have studied the text. We meditate on God's Torah in both the text and in life around us. The psalm then places before the reader two metaphors, a choice: do you want to be a fruitful tree or chaff blown by the wind? Those who delight in God's teaching are like a tree. Those who choose the other way are like chaff. We the readers must make the choice: do I wish to be a flourishing tree or dead chaff? The other, lesser, metaphor in this psalm is 'way' or 'path'. This too is associated with the choice the reader is invited to make: what path will I choose?

To sum it up, Psalm 1 invites the reader into the whole array of the book. It invites the reader to be a happy person, to make choices, to delight in God's teachings and to see oneself as a tree planted near a running stream. However, it does this through contrasting metaphors and the choice as to the path or direction for life. It is somewhat confronting in its dualism, the either/or nature of the choice: there is no grey here, only black or white. It therefore suggests that the remainder of the Psalter will continue to teach us about our choices and God's ways. There may be grey areas in life, but the Psalter deals more with the emotional highs and lows, helping us discern the meaning of our experience by placing before us the extremes.

Psalm 1 sets us on a path to explore the Psalter through paying attention to its details, message, poetry and starkness.

Like the Torah, the Psalter is divided into five books. The Torah (or Pentateuch) has a special place in Judaism and the psalms reflect this by their five-fold division, indicating that the Psalter has a similar authority and importance for the life of the people of Israel. This will be explored later.

We have seen how Psalm 1 invites us into the whole Book of Psalms; it is a Torah psalm. Torah psalms are focused on God's teachings, God's *Torah*. They praise these teachings and commandments and notice the great wisdom in them. The longest psalm in the Psalter, Psalm 119, is also a Torah psalm; it is 176 verses long and in earlier times many Christian scholars called it boring. It is an acrostic psalm: based on the Hebrew alphabet, it is an outpouring of appreciation and love for the *Torah* and for the God who teaches and instructs the psalmist how to live according to God's ways. It says everything from A to Z – or in the Hebrew alphabet, everything from *aleph* to *tav*.

God's teachings, elaborated in Psalm 119, are the path to happiness for this psalmist, as suggested in Psalm 1 and celebrated in Psalm 19 (the third of the *Torah* psalms).

> Did you know that the Hebrew word *Torah* is usually translated as 'law', but this is a limited interpretation that does not reflect *Torah's* range of meaning? *Torah* can refer to the first five books of the Bible and also to all of God's teachings. Both these interpretations include laws as well as the kind of teachings offered by God through story, invitations and direct speech. In this work I will not translate *Torah* but retain the Hebrew transliteration.

The psalm then places before the reader two metaphors, a choice:
do you want to be a fruitful tree or chaff blown by the wind?
Those who delight in God's teaching are like a tree.
Those who choose the other way are like chaff.

Psalms and Life — Then and Now

The Book of Psalms helps us give expression to what we are feeling in words from long ago, words that have passed the test of time for more than 2000 years. Psalms help us to make meaning of our own experiences as we give voice to our pain and joy, our anger and thanksgiving. The psalms invite us to speak to God in the rawness of pain or the elation of wonder. In doing so we understand ourselves better, and deepen our relationship with God.

Life: Oriented, Disoriented and Re-oriented

The renowned American biblical scholar Walter Brueggemann has found inspiration in the way that the psalms can help us articulate the full range of human experience. He was particularly drawn to the lament psalms, as he felt that Christian tradition has not engaged with these, leaving it insufficiently alert to the pain in life and the related social justice issues. The laments, by contrast, give full voice to these issues.

Brueggemann was prompted by the writings of the philosopher Paul Ricœur to see patterns in the psalms – patterns of *orientation, disorientation* and *reorientation*.

Brueggemann's way of seeing patterns in the psalms offers a simple way to view the movements in life, our major disruptions and changes. It is a helpful way of reflecting on life through the ancient texts of the psalms. We know that we are not really in control of our lives; changes cause upheavals: a death of a beloved, the loss of a job, sudden illness or even a pandemic. These disorienting events disrupt our 'normal' lives: our oriented lives become disoriented, and it will be some time before we find a new normal, a reoriented life.

Brueggemann is especially interested in the lament psalms, for if we have forgotten how to lament then we may not be alert to prompts within and around us – prompts to notice what is wrong around us and to act justly, to be aware of injustices and to respond to them in prayer and action. Ignoring our own personal pain does not cure it; it needs to find expression and the laments provide a means for this.

> יהוה
>
> YHWH, God's particular name is composed of four letters in Hebrew, the tetragrammaton. 'YHWH' is the way that the most sacred name of the God of Israel is rendered. It was revealed to Moses at a time when there were many gods acknowledged in the Ancient Near East (ANE). It is a way of speaking which indicates a personal relationship, on a first-name basis, and yet the reverence in not pronouncing this name indicates how special it was, and continues to be.
>
> Israel spoke of God's name dwelling in the Temple. This was a way of remembering how present God was to them and Psalm 8 speaks of God's majestic name in all the earth. The particularity of the Temple and the universality of the heavens are a way of saying God is here and is everywhere. In Judaism, people call God *HaShem* (the name) thereby making oblique reference to this very sacred name. In the NRSV translation this name is indicated by the use of capital letters for the word LORD. Thus YHWH = LORD. Any other use of lord/Lord in the NRSV represents a different Hebrew word.

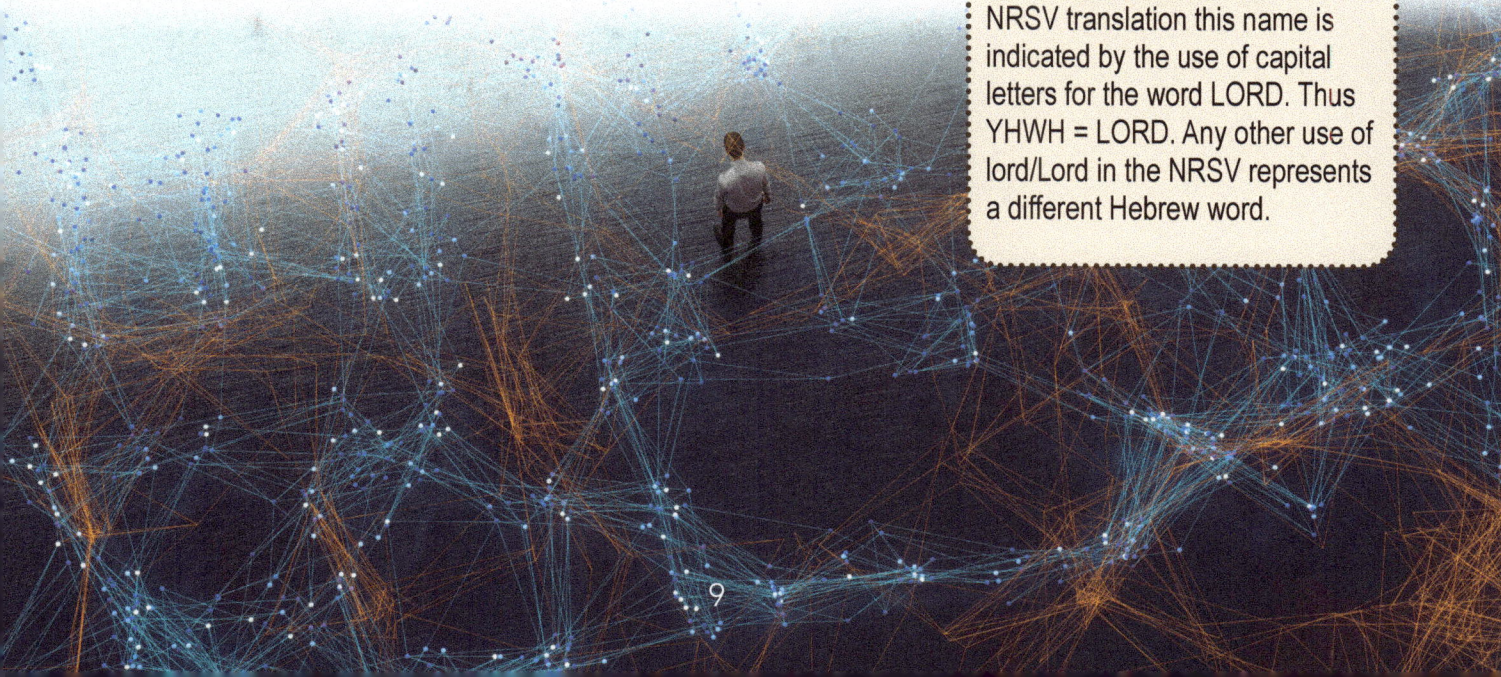

> **Hesed**
> The word is often translated as 'steadfast love'. It is the foundation of the covenant; it is God's love for Israel and also their responding love. It is theologically and biblically the most common descriptor for God. In Christian traditions we have generally understood covenant as a wide, universal covenant, as promised in the Book of Isaiah and in the letters of Paul. In Jewish thinking, a reference to the covenant is normally to the Sinai covenant unless otherwise specified.
>
> The enduring nature of *hesed*, especially on God's part, depicts God's reliability. *Hesed* is often translated as 'kindness' but to my mind it is stronger than kindness: it is a love that is steadfast, enduring and reliable. The people who enter into covenant with YHWH are asked to be as faithful to the covenant as is God. But mortals are not God and God's *hesed* is unfailing even in the face of neglect or rejection.

This recognition that life has times of orientation, disorientation and reorientation can help us to go to psalms that give expression to our current state. The psalms can also remind us of others: my sisters and brothers elsewhere may be suffering trauma and when I pray a psalm of disorientation, even if my life is fine, I can pray with and for them.

ORIENTATION

PSALM 8
To the leader: according to The Gittith. A Psalm of David.

When I am living an ordered, somewhat predictable existence, I may wish to pray Psalm 8. This text is easy for many of us to identify with. It asks a fundamental question: *What are human beings that you are mindful of them?* (8:4) Is our God remote, or as this psalm suggests, does God care for us, collectively and personally? The psalmist implies a very positive 'yes' – the text continues: *you have made them a little lower than God* (8:5). The opening and concluding refrain is a direct address to God, who is named with the particular name YHWH and is experienced as Sovereign.

This psalm is about me as a human being, but even more so about God, the sovereign Lord of all, whose majesty is reflected in all the earth and in the heavens. We know the experience of standing before a star-studded sky and being overwhelmed by its beauty and immensity. Psalm 8 captures that experience for us and invites self-reflection.

The puniness of self when faced with the vastness of God's creation seems to almost overwhelm the psalmist. Yet there is also wonder, that the human person, the puny me, is also marvellous and godly. This is a paradox, and makes us ask: am I of no consequence or am I godly?

The whole psalm is bracketed by the refrain: *O LORD, our sovereign, how majestic is your name in all the earth* (8:1 & 9) The refrain reminds the reader of the one who is truly mighty. There is both familiarity and otherness in the psalm and especially the refrain, in which the One I know by name is the 'Ruler of the Earth'.

DISORIENTATION

If my life feels like chaos and I am disoriented, I may use the words of Psalm 13 or Psalm 44 to give expression to my feelings and to tell God what I am experiencing. Psalm 13 is dark and to some extent shocking. Yet the honesty of the relationship with God is clear and true. *How long, O Lord? Will you forget me forever?* (13:1) How often have I experienced this feeling of being abandoned by God? This may be on occasions of serious illness, a couple waiting and hoping to conceive a child, times of war, famine or drought. These are the words of someone in a time of severe disorientation.

The expression of pain is called a *lament* and it:
- addresses God
- speaks of the intense pain
- asks God to change things and
- promises to *sing to the Lord* when things improve.

The relationship with God is raw and real: this is what is happening to me, God – and I do not understand why you are not intervening on my behalf.

Psalm 13
To the leader. A psalm of David.

Psalm 13 speaks of an enemy. In fact, many psalms mention enemies. These may be people with whom Israel was at war; neighbours who are being difficult; others who see important things differently to the psalmist or the enemy may be within. The enemy may also be circumstances beyond the control of the psalmist: loss, death, illness, loneliness, depression, famine, war, homelessness, injustice. In Psalm 13, it is other people but we are not told the nature of their 'looming' over the psalmist or overcoming him. The threat by these enemies is real and prolonged and yet not named specifically.

The imagery in most psalms is general and this may be intentional; what we know is that it allows us to interpret metaphors like enemies for our reality today. Psalm 13 is an ancient prayer but we know today the intense suffering involved in feeling overcome by the injustices around us and the conflicts within us. Psalm 13 is in the singular, a psalm spoken by an individual. Other laments are clearly spoken on behalf of the community.

Psalm 44
To the leader. Of the Korahites. A Maskil.

Psalm 44 is a communal lament. It is also classified as a 'psalm of innocence'. The community is perplexed because it has not been untrue to God's ways and yet it is suffering. There was a theology that understood suffering as a consequence

---

The Structure of Psalm 13

Verses 1–2
'How long' is repeated 4 times. Addressed to LORD, which is the sacred name in Hebrew YHWH.

The suffering is within, in the soul and heart, even though the threat is external. The suffering is primarily due to the lack of response on God's part and in a secondary way the oppression by the enemies.

Verses 3–4
Prayer
A request to God to respond – to consider and answer. A long wait is imagined between these sections.

Verses 5–6
Although the tenses in English are clear, in Hebrew it is more ambiguous. It can be understood that God has responded or the confidence that God will respond. The grounds for confidence is God's *hesed*.

The Structure of Psalm 44

Verses 1–3
Addresses God and remembers the past

Verses 4–16
Speaks of the intense pain in the present

Verses 17–22
Protests innocence in the present

Verses 23–26
Urges God to change things in the present.

> **Covenant**
> The covenant with God is a mutual agreement, which requires commitment and response from both parties. In the Old Testament there are several covenants. One with Noah for all of humanity and all creatures (Gen 9); one with Abraham for his descendants (Gen 17); one with Moses for the people of Israel, the Sinai covenant (Ex 19); another with David and his descendants for all the people of Israel (2 Sam 7:12–16); one in Jeremiah where a new covenant is envisaged as the people have disregarded the Mosaic covenant (Jer 31:31–34).
>
> Frequently, references to the covenant are to the Mosaic covenant, although the covenant with David is commonly mentioned in the psalms. The basis of these covenants, and especially the Mosaic covenant, is God's *hesed* and it asks for a similar steadfast love from the people. Scholars today are clear that these are all expressions of one covenant by God with Israel and with humanity.

of acting contrary to God's ways; yet their current situation did not fit this theology. I suspect we experience this dilemma when we see thousands of refugees being rejected or imprisoned; or when we learn of the fate of those trapped in a bushfire. We know it is not because they have sinned but is an outcome of tragic circumstances beyond their control.

Psalm 44 begins with an unusual sentence: *We have heard with our ears, O God, our ancestors have told us, what deeds you performed in their days, in the days of old.* (44:1) This psalm is addressed to God; it is recalling the traditions of Israel, which have been handed on probably within a liturgical context. The particular tradition which this psalm recalls then becomes clear: that of Israel being planted in the biblical land by God. (This tradition is expanded in Ps 80:8–19.)

Psalm 44:4–8 then unveils the reason this tradition is being remembered. This section focuses on the times God has been with them in battles and God's presence has been the source of their victories. *For not in my bow do I trust, nor can my sword save me. But you have saved us from our foes.* This marvellous confidence relates to the past, the way God had acted in former times. The next section (44: 9–16) makes the dilemma clear: *Yet you have rejected us and abased us, and you have not gone out with our armies.* We are losing battles and you, O God, do not seem to be on our side; you are not with us in our present as you were in the past.

The plot intensifies as verse 17 reveals: *All this has come upon us, yet we have not forgotten you, or been false to your covenant.* We are innocent, we have been faithful to the covenant and you, God, do not seem to be being faithful. The anguish, the fear, maybe even anger is clear. If God cannot be relied on, if God forgets promises and the covenant, what is reliable in life? God has forgotten us even though we have not forgotten God.

Then the actual petition is uttered: *Rouse yourself! Why do you sleep, O LORD? Awake, do not cast us off forever! Why do you hide your face?* (44:23-24) The people's hope is that God will act; they envisage God being asleep because the alternative (that God has abandoned them) is beyond belief.

The final sentence makes their hope clear: *Redeem us for the sake of your steadfast love.* The text uses the word *hesed*. Their hope is in the essence of who God is, *hesed*. The threat which defeat in war implies is loss of the land. This is why they were remembering the stories of God leading them into the land. Now the enemies threaten their security in the land and they are bewildered.

This lament gives full voice to the pain of the people as they experience defeat in war, but much more fundamentally it expresses their bewilderment at God's inaction on their behalf. They have been true to God, but it seems that God has not reciprocated. The covenant is in question, the foundational relationship is threatened. Yet it is to their covenantal partner that they turn – there is nowhere else to go!

And so, they pray to the one they fear is not listening, is asleep. This is

the hope that times of disorientation offer. The truth this psalm articulates is profound. It is not a truth of doctrine but the depth of relationship which cannot be relinquished even when it seems God has abandoned them.

The lament psalms, psalms of disorientation, invite us to give full expression to suffering, to penitence, to abandonment, to disorientation. Through praying these deep sorrows, we find the core of our relationship with God, our faith in the one who sometimes seems remote. The one we can plead with, cajole, yell at, but never let go: the source and ground of our hope.

REORIENTATION

Some time after suffering an emotional, physical, psychological or spiritual blow or upheaval, we may find that equilibrium has returned to our lives. It may take days, years, even decades. This is the reorientation/new orientation to which Brueggemann refers. Psalm 30 gives expression to this time in life. It is not the same as a psalm of orientation: life is not the same as before, but neither is it the raw suffering of the laments. Many of these psalms are *thanksgiving* psalms.

PSALM 30
A Psalm. A Song at the dedication of the temple. Of David.

Psalm 30 begins with an expression by the psalmist, exalting God. We, the reader, wonder why. Immediately, we are told that God has drawn the psalmist up. What does this mean? It becomes clear as the psalm progresses and we learn that he has been saved 'from the pit'.

The pit is both an image of and metaphor for death. God has drawn the psalmist up from enemies and the threat of death; literally or symbolically. This person has recovered from the disorientation which is described especially in verses 8-10. This psalm can appear naïve at first reading, or overly pious.

It is the prayer of someone who has faced serious trauma: it has the ring of truth and authenticity as the traumatised narrator keeps going over the events, something common to PTSD sufferers. The lament, the terrifying experience, is referred to several times, and it contrasts with the new moment. The present and the past continue to interact.

There is also a focus on the one who has saved the psalmist: *you have … you have … you have …* The gratitude is palpable. This psalm is a dialogue, first with God and (in verses 4–5) with the wider community. The change the person has experienced is perhaps best expressed in the words: *you have turned my mourning into dancing* (verse 11).

The new orientation is a time of remembering, of dancing and of deep gratitude.

However, there is another movement in this psalm; it begins in the present but moves quickly to remember the distress only to return to the present and the experience of healing and restoration. In verse 5 there is a glimpse towards the future: *God's anger is but for a moment, God's favour is for a lifetime.* This glimpse becomes clearer in the final verse: *O LORD my God, I will give thanks to you forever.* This psalm is not the words of a naïve optimist, it is the outpouring of a healed and restored disciple who commits to a future of gratitude.

OUR LIVED EXPERIENCES

Whichever situation in life you find yourself in today, there is a psalm to help you give expression to what you are feeling and experiencing. Beyond the personal, the psalms act as a reminder that others are at different times in their lives: I can join in solidarity with those who rejoice, even while I suffer; or empathise with those who struggle, even while I am safe and secure.

We are called in prayer to give expression both to our own reality and to that of our sisters and brothers in other places and other circumstances. Brueggemann's three-fold movement is a helpful way to link these ancient prayers with our life today.

Genres in Psalms

> ### Main genres of psalms
>
> #### Psalms of lament
>
> - Invoking God
> - Description of sorrow or pain
> - Plea or prayer for change
> - Promise to do something when the plea is answered.
>
> #### Hymns
>
> - Call to praise
> - Reasons for praise
> - Final call to praise.
>
> #### Thanksgiving psalms
>
> - Expression of thanks to God
> - A remembrance of the distress
> - An acknowledgement that things have changed
> - A recognition that the change is attributed to God.

We are used to different genres in music: country music, classical music, rock, reggae, pop. In literature we also encounter different styles which bear certain characteristics: comics, manuals, novels, biographies, tweets, memos, textbooks, cookery books and more.

Psalms also have their own genres: laments, hymns, thanksgiving psalms, wisdom psalms, and liturgies. Each genre has its characteristic structure, content, mood and in some cases its social context of origin.

Previously, we examined one form of categorisation: orientation, disorientation and reorientation. These align with the *three* most common genres in the Psalter:

- hymns
- laments
- thanksgiving psalms.

The lament is the most frequent genre in the Psalter. However, as we move through the Psalter the number of hymns increases until we reach the last psalm, which is an outpouring of praise and ends in a final invitation: *Let everything that breathes praise the LORD! Praise the LORD!* (Ps 150:6).

Biblical hymns are essentially expressions of praise and are related to thanksgiving psalms. Both are concerned with praise; but thanksgiving psalms are related to laments in their structure and aspects of their content. A thanksgiving psalm essentially remembers the 'cause of the pain' and then proceeds to 'thank God for the change in circumstances.' There are also less-common genres which will be mentioned but not examined in detail.

Knowing the genre of a psalm helps us to approach it better, to know what to look for and how to understand the parts in relation to the whole. It can also help us look at psalms in relation to each other. There is nothing absolute about naming the genre, it is simply a way to know what to expect, to note deviations from the norm and to read in an informed manner.

Lament Genre

Lament psalms, sometimes called complaints, are both communal and individual (although some of them in the singular may be representative and therefore communal in intent).

The 'nature' of the suffering affects the particularity of a lament. If the suffering comes from a sense of guilt then it will be a penitential lament; if it comes from external sources, such as oppression or attacks by enemies, then it may describe the pain or express a sense of being abandoned by God.

All the laments in the Psalter ask for, and anticipate, a response from God; if, as we saw with Psalm 44, the people feel they have been faithful to the covenant and God is not upholding his side of the agreement, we will notice that there is no promise or vow at the end of the psalm.

Questions are common in laments: *How long, O God? Why? When?* Do we not also ask these questions when we suffer, or when we see on the news that thousands are starving, or that lives are being ravaged by wars, or that those close by are being harmed by bush fires or pandemics. *Why? How long?* These laments encourage us to ask such questions and even give us models for articulating them in bold terms. This is because laments are expressed within a deep and steadfast relationship. The Israelites dared to utter bold questions and they encourage us Jews and Christians of today to be as forthright in our relationship with God as were our forebears.

The other remarkable thing about laments is their variety. Just as life has all sorts of sorrows, so there is a similar range of laments. There are six penitential psalms of which the best known is Psalm 51 (50). It begins: *Have mercy on me O God, according to your steadfast love ...* It begs for God's mercy and recalls *hesed* as the dominant characteristic of God and therefore anticipates that God will act again in accord with *hesed*.

Above: Musicians playing the lyre, psaltery and drum, from the Utrecht Psalter circa 850 CE

Psalm 51
To the leader. A Psalm of David, when the prophet Nathan came to him, after he had gone in to Bathsheba.

Psalm 51 is a very familiar individual lament. Like many psalms, it has a superscription, a heading. This

> When recognising certain genres we anticipate that they will have similar content, structure, mood and come from a related social context. This helps us to approach the particular psalm with certain presuppositions and questions.

> **Superscriptions**
> These are found on more than 100 of the psalm texts. They are part of the Hebrew text and therefore part of the Scriptures. They probably belong to a stage in the editing of what is now the Psalter. They link psalms with historical figures like King David, and include some liturgical clues and indications of psalm types. These headings are brief and often obscure. The three most common links to figures are to David, to Asaph and to Korah.
>
> The liturgical clues in the superscription are thought to be associated with the use of the psalms in the second Temple in Jerusalem. *Lamnasseh* is in the heading of 55 psalms and is translated *to the leader*, a reference to a liturgical leader or even conductor. Other terms relate to musical instruments and liturgical indications. The psalm types *mizmor* (psalm) and *shir* (song) also reveal clues about liturgical usage. These are to be distinguished from the headings added by modern editors.

heading links the psalm with David; the link is very specific to a time in David's life. This was the time when King David sinned greatly, when he had a sexual relationship with another man's wife and then had the husband killed to hide his sin. This story is related in 2 Samuel 11–12. When David is confronted by the prophet Nathan for his wrong doing he responds: *I have sinned against the LORD*. David is portrayed as a sinner who acknowledges his wrongdoing and he certainly could have prayed this psalm. The link with King David will be discussed later.

In Christian tradition it is one of the seven penitential psalms (Psalms 6, 32, 38, 51, 102, 130, and 143). This psalm laments sin and offences committed by the psalmist, launching straight into this concern. The writer readily admits guilt but this is not the focus – rather, it is the desire for God's mercy, which will wash clean the guilt. In one sense the emphasis is on God who is characterised as *hesed* and one of great compassion.

Many other laments speak of enemies, or defeat in battle. This time the enemy is 'within' and acknowledged, the regret gives rise to a desire to be forgiven and then to act differently. It lacks the usual complaint against others or even self, but in its own way it has the basic elements of a lament: it invokes God, describes the pain of guilt, asks God to change the individual's reality through forgiveness and mercy and finally promises to *declare your praise* (v 15).

As we come to the last four verses, things seem to change. Verses 16–17 are unexpected and ponder more the nature of proper sacrifice; these verses are not anti-sacrifice but are musing upon the disposition which must accompany right sacrifice – a broken and contrite spirit. This is not an abused spirit, but one which is open to God's ways, a truly humble spirit, willing to receive God's mercy. The last two verses (18–19) many say are a later addition; these are linked through the word 'sacrifice' but take a very different direction.

The psalm now turns to Zion, Jerusalem, the place of sacrifice par excellence and prays for its restoration. This is possibly an addition arising from the experience of the Babylonian Exile and the accompanying destruction of Jerusalem. Yet it is now an accepted component of the biblical text.

Below: King David watching Bathsheba bathe by James Tissot, 1836–1902

Hymns

In the Psalter, hymns are essentially praise of God. Sometimes God is praised as Creator, at other times for the wonders God has performed in the life of Israel. These are times when God's acts of salvation and goodness are remembered or experienced. God is also praised via the holy city, Zion, which is the place where God dwells. Finally, there are hymns that praise God as king. The hymns have a very simple structure: a call to praise and then a longer section enumerating the aspects to be praised and concluding with an echo of the initial call to praise.

Psalm 97

Psalm 97 is a hymn praising God as king. It begins with the cry: *The LORD is king! Let the earth rejoice.* We note that it is not only humans who rejoice in God's kingship but all of the earth. When God reigns, everything is in balance.

In our day of environmental crises, we are reminded that God is king of the whole earth, the whole cosmos, and God's reign is manifest when all aspects of creation contribute to life for the whole created order and are respected for their contribution. We see God praised by the way the whole of creation responds to the manifestation, or theophany, of God. Clouds, darkness, fire, lightning, mountains: all respond to the presence of the king of the whole created order.

The beautiful parallel in verse 6 has the heavens proclaiming God's righteousness and humans beholding God's glory. This is a wonderful imagining of the mutuality between humanity and the rest of the creation. The text suggests that the heavens speak and humanity sees. The created order is not merely a silent witness: it proclaims God's presence but we need ears that can hear. We humans behold the glory around us and in that instant, we see God.

This psalm is thought to have been written for a feast where God was symbolically enthroned as king. The enthronement psalms are Psalms 47 and 93–99. The background to this feast possibly lies in a Babylonian feast wherein the god Marduk was enthroned. This is told in the Babylonian document *Enuma Elish*, a copy of which was found in excavations near Nineveh in 1875.

The opening invitation to rejoice is addressed to the earth and the distant coast lands. God's enthronement is portrayed in terms of clouds, darkness and fire and is reminiscent of descriptions in Exodus 19 and Isaiah 6. The throne-room is cosmic and all the earth responds: the mountains and the heavens recognise the presence of God. Then the focus moves to Zion – from the universal to the particular within a few verses. This universal king is also the judge who guards, rescues and brings light to the righteous. The final invitation is to give thanks to this holy one, to God's holy name.

This psalm mentions the foundation of God's throne as righteousness and justice in verse 2, then justice is proclaimed by the heavens in verse 6, and later in verse 11, light dawns for the just and finally, in verse 12, the just are invited to rejoice in the Lord. Thus, this hymn which praises God with all of creation, also declares that the God of justice will not allow injustice to hold sway forever. In this sense God comes to judge, and in doing so, to set things right.

Mythic Background and Language

A number of psalms show evidence of imagery, vocabulary and even theological concepts that are influenced by Israel's neighbours and speak in mythological language. This language speaks of what happens in the heavenly realm so as to understand why things are as they are on the earthly sphere. There are myths about how creation took place and one of these is reflected in Psalm 74:12–14.

Israel's neighbours had their own gods; several biblical texts acknowledge this and then proclaim the superiority of Israel's God. This is not pure monotheism but is a background to what became monotheism.

Psalm 97 reflects another aspect of the mythology of Israel's neighbours. It is the story of the annual enthronement of Marduk, a Babylonian god, so as to honour *Marduk* and proclaim his superiority. These stories are not literally true, but were the best explanations they had in their day. Thus, the enthronement psalms of Israel have this influence from their neighbours and belong in a liturgical context where Israel proclaimed the superiority of its God.

Right: Marduk on Babylonian relief

Common elements of thanksgiving psalms:

- Expression of thanks to God
- A remembrance of the distress
- An acknowledgement that things have changed
- A recognition that the change is attributed to God.

Thanksgiving Psalms

There are only a few thanksgiving psalms, among them 30, 34 and 138. They are related to hymns, as thanks and praise come from a similar movement within the individual and communal heart. This genre recalls the situation from which there has been a release, and in this it has similarities to laments.

The gratitude is for the change of circumstances: after the pain there is a newness, a new orientation in life. These psalms do not forget the pain but they are no longer in the place where the pain dominates. They are thankful for the change, the healing, the new life.

Psalm 118

This psalm is a lovely example of a thanksgiving psalm. It is both individual and communal. It has several links to a liturgical context where one voice is speaking but it represents the community gathered in worship to give thanks. The psalm opens with the call to give thanks to the Lord who is good and who is characterised by mercy.

The liturgical context becomes clear as Israel, gathered as the whole congregation, is first invited to offer thanks; then the house of Aaron representing the priests, and finally a group called the God-fearers (possibly a group who desired to enter the community) is invited to join in the song of thanksgiving. The same groups are mentioned in Psalm 115.

Verses 5–9 make it clear that the psalmist found that mortals failed him and that only God was a reliable helper. Verses 10–18 use dramatic language to portray the battle in which he was engaged. Finally verses 19–29 represent a liturgy of thanksgiving to celebrate this change brought about by God. In verse 22, the psalmist is *the stone that the builders rejected (which) has become the chief cornerstone*.

This confident claim represents a dramatic experience of being saved from overwhelming threat. This text is familiar, as it is quoted in Mark 12:10. This outpouring of thanksgiving affirms that *this is the LORD's doing; it is marvellous in our eyes*. Thus, the gratitude for the saving act is directed wholly to God.

Less Common Genres

There are several genres which only occur a few times and they need to be mentioned but cannot be explored here. They are:

1. **Wisdom psalms**, which aim to teach rather than being a prayer. They sometimes look at life's questions and see wisdom reflected in nature, especially the harmony in the natural order. They resemble the Wisdom books: Proverbs, Job, Ecclesiastes, Sirach and Wisdom. Examples: Psalms 14, 37, 49, 73.

2. **Torah psalms**, which are associated with wisdom but focus specifically on the wisdom of God's teaching, in *Torah*. Examples: Psalms 1, 19, 119.

3. **Liturgies**, which are psalms that are a liturgical rite in themselves. Good examples are Psalms 15 & 24, which mirror an entrance liturgy.

4. **Historical psalms**, which retell aspects of the history of Israel. Psalm 78 is the clearest example and is the second longest psalm in the Psalter. It may be interesting to know that it contains the middle verse of the Psalter! Examples: 78, 105, 106, 135, 136.

5. **Royal psalms**, which focus on the king, especially the Davidic king. The king was anointed and therefore the word *messiah* is used in relation to the Davidic king who was anointed when he became king and entered into the ongoing covenant with God, which promised that a Davidic king would always be on the throne of Israel and Judah. The early Christian community used these psalms to speak of Jesus as anointed of the line of David, a *messiah*. Some examples are Psalms 2, 21, 110.

6. **Zion psalms**, which praise God by praising the city, Zion or Jerusalem, which houses God's name in the Temple and in which God's throne is established. Examples: 46, 48, 122.

Above middle: praying at the Western Wall; bottom: King David playing the Harp by Gerard van Honthorst, 1622

THE BOOKS OF THE PSALTER

The Psalter is divided into five books, via the use of doxologies, and, as aforementioned, most scholars agree that this is in imitation of the Torah/Pentateuch, the first 5 books of the Bible. The end of each book is marked by a doxology as can be seen in the box opposite. The doxologies are short statements of praise found at the end of each of the five books. These doxologies vary somewhat but are recognisable, and while regarded as part of the last psalm of each book they do stand out from the flow of the psalm.

An example may assist: *Blessed be the LORD, the God of Israel, from everlasting to everlasting. Amen and Amen.* Ps 41:13. This blessing is unexpected at the end of Psalm 41, which is a lament.

Earlier we looked at structures within particular psalms; in a related manner, the structure of the Psalter also conveys meaning. This meaning is about the role of the Psalter in Israel's evolving story.

The five-fold division of the Psalter tells us that this somehow parallels the foundational story, found in the first five books of the Bible. It suggests that the prayers and teachings of the Psalter are as foundational to the life of Israel as is the Torah/Pentateuch.

Psalm 1 has already introduced the Psalter as a source of happiness and teachings about living a good life; this too can be said of the Torah/Pentateuch. The five-fold structure of the Psalter is very late in its formation, at a time when the link would have been obvious, which it isn't to many Christians today. It invites us to know our past, the stories and teachings of the Torah/Pentateuch, so as to live well the present.

Below: Reading from the Torah, Jerusalem

The 5 books of the Psalter and their doxologies

BOOK	PSALMS	DOXOLOGY
One	Psalms 1–41	Blessed be the LORD, the God of Israel, from everlasting to everlasting. Amen and Amen.
Two	Psalms 42–72	Blessed be the LORD, the God of Israel, who alone does wondrous things. Blessed be his glorious name for ever; may his glory fill the whole earth. Amen and Amen. The prayers of David son of Jesse are ended. * *Psalm 72 has this strange comment: *The prayers of David son of Jesse are ended.* It implies that all of the Davidic psalms are in Psalms 1–72, yet this is not so. It is an unusual editorial comment, probably from an early stage in the growth of the Psalter.
Three	Psalms 73–89	Blessed be the LORD for ever. Amen and Amen.
Four	Psalms 90–106	Blessed be the LORD, the God of Israel, from everlasting to everlasting. And let all the people say, 'Amen.' Praise the LORD!
Five	Psalms 107–150	The concluding doxology is the whole of Psalm 150 and some scholars say that it is Psalms 146–150.

The Dead Sea Scrolls

This five-fold nature of the Psalter also reveals something of its growth and how it was an instrument in the developing theology of Israel. When the Dead Sea Scrolls were discovered, between 1947 and 1956, they witnessed to the accuracy of the scribes as they copied the scrolls over hundreds of years. The Dead Sea Scrolls also show some textual differences, especially in relation to psalm texts.

The scrolls were found in eleven caves over approximately ten years. They had been hidden in clay pots about 2000 years ago, when the community of Essenes was overwhelmed by the Roman army in the place we call Qumran, on the edge of the Dead Sea, an extremely dry and minimally inhabited place.

The scrolls lay dormant for all those years and were initially discovered by young Bedouin shepherds. When unravelled and eventually read, some of the partial psalm manuscripts seemed to have the psalms of Books 4 and 5 in an order different from previously known copies. Thus began a scholarly search to find the shape of the Psalter and its story and theology.

There is a dominance of laments in the first three books of the Psalter and a greater concentration of hymns in Books 4 and 5. Thus, in general, there is a movement from lament to praise but this is not consistent or regular. There is also a greater focus on King David in the first three books and statements at the end of Book 3, which address the seeming loss of a reigning Davidic king. Towards the end of Book 3, in Ps 89:49, we read an example of this: *Lord, where is*

Below left to right: satellite image of the Dead Sea showing Qumran; Qumran caves; storage jars; part of Dead Sea Scroll 28a from Qumran

your steadfast love of old, which by your faithfulness you swore to David?

This raises the question of God's reliability, because the promise to David was understood to be everlasting. However, from the beginning of Book 4 there is an increase in references to God's kingship. Thus, many scholars postulate that Books 1–3 were formed earlier than Books 4–5. It is suggested that the Psalter was reshaped in response to the growing acceptance that a Davidic king would not be reinstated in the post-Babylonian Exile period. Thus, theologically the emphasis moved to God's faithful rule, not mediated by an earthly Davidic king, but through a reaffirmation of the fact that God is Israel's true king.

This does not mean that every psalm within a book is composed at the same time; in fact, the Psalter grew, possibly over hundreds of years. It is the final shaping and editing which imposed the five-fold division. Many psalms were preserved within this structure and retain their original theology even while being placed into the five-fold structure of the final form of the Psalter. The Psalter has several sub-groups, which are mainly indicated by words within the superscriptions which actually belong to the text of the psalm. (I do not refer to headings supplied by modern editors).

There are collections associated with Korah, Asaph, David and Psalms of Ascent. The more we delve into the shape of the Psalter the more we learn about the care with which the ancient editors shared the psalms with their contemporaries. We are the recipients of this care, its story and theology.

BOOK 1

1
2
3–41: David

BOOK 2

42–49: Korah
50: Asaph
51–72: David

BOOK 3

73–83: Asaph
84–89: Korah and others

BOOK 4

90
91
92
93–100: Kingship
101: David
102
103: David
104–106: Hallel

BOOK 5

107
108–110: David
111
112–118: Hallel
119
120–134: Ascents
135
136
137
138–145: David
146–150: Hallel

Meet God through Imagery

Most psalms are prayers in their most basic form. They are part of a dialogue with the one who is the people's hope, sometimes their last resort, but also their rock, their redeemer, their creator, the one whose name dwells in all the earth. I can also say: my rock, my redeemer, my creator.

Psalms are typically addressed to God; a few talk about God, some even quote God's words. There is not a psalm in the Psalter which does not speak to God or about God. These texts are an expression of the I-Thou relationship of which Martin Buber spoke. St Athanasius of Alexandria, who died in 373 CE, wrote a letter to his friend Marcellinus in which he said many things about the psalms. Two of his comments are very pertinent: 'Most of the scripture speaks to us; the psalms speak for us' and 'A psalm is a mirror in which you contemplate yourself and the movements of your soul'.

These comments are another way of reminding us that the psalms belong in a context of dialogue between human beings and God but that they also help us look inwards into our own person. Thus, the dialogues include self-reflection both before and after speaking. Self-reflection, an internal dialogue, offers the possibility of growth and newness. Our dialogues are both personal and communal, with self, the community and with God.

The God who is addressed in the psalms is characterised by *hesed* and mercy and justice. It is the God who is in a covenantal relationship with Israel, and through the Jewish Jesus, with Christians too. The psalms are uttered within a deep relationship with the one who is 'other' and yet who is known intimately and who allows the speakers to speak their truth.

Following is a brief exploration of four images for God found in the psalms.

Midwife

There is an image of God in the Psalms which is not found often in the Scriptures and is worth attending to. In two psalms we see God depicted as a midwife.

There are only two other biblical texts which use this beautiful metaphor: (Job 10:18 and Isaiah 66:9). They are all poetic texts and take the concept of God as creator and life giver. They shine a different light by portraying God as the one who assists at the psalmist's birth (and thereby at our own birth) and who receives us as we come from our mother's womb. This is a moment of helplessness and threat, but God is there to receive us, ensuring our safe passage from the womb to be held and then given to our mothers.

> *Yet it was you who took me from the womb;*
> *you kept me safe on my mother's breast. Ps 22:9*

> *Upon you I have leaned from my birth;*
> *it was you who took me from my mother's womb.*
> *My praise is continually of you. Ps 71:6.*

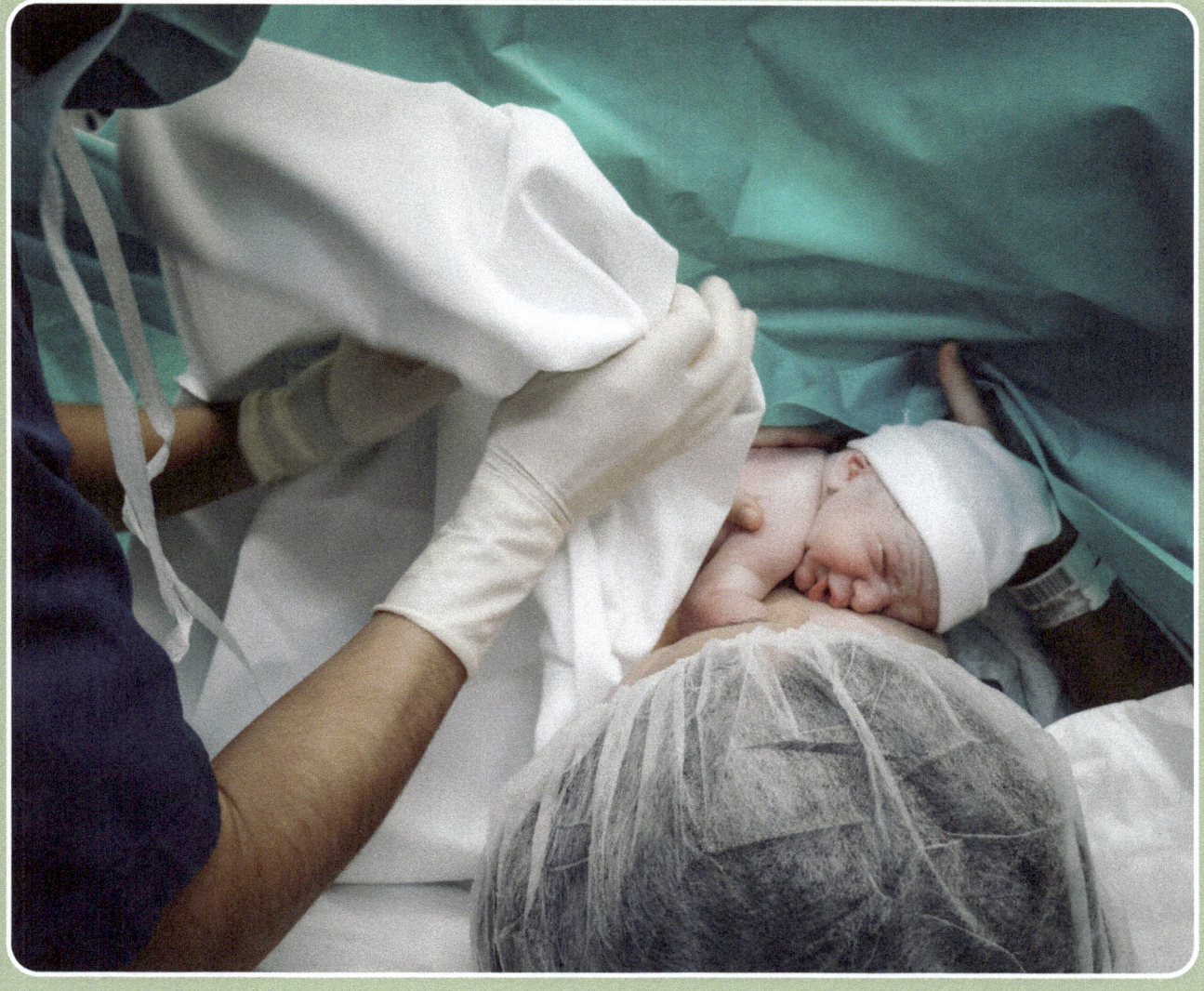

Creator

It has been said that the first act of salvation is in fact Creation. We are saved from non-existence and called into life and relationships. Several psalms speak of God as Creator and remind us of just how inclusive this is; it is not only we humans who are created but the cosmos and it is not only we humans who respond to the Creator. The following texts offer a sample:

- *The heavens are telling the glory of God; and
  the firmament proclaims his handiwork.*
  Ps 19:1
- *The earth is the LORD's and all that is in it,
  the world, and those who live in it;
  for he has founded it on the seas,
  and established it on the rivers.*
  Ps 24:1–2
- *By the word of the LORD the heavens were made,
  and all their host by the breath of his mouth.
  He gathered the waters of the sea as in a bottle;
  he put the deeps in storehouses.*
- *Let all the earth fear the LORD;
  let all the inhabitants of the world stand in awe of him.
  For he spoke, and it came to be;
  he commanded, and it stood firm.*
  Ps 33:6–9
- *Know that the LORD is God.
  It is he that made us, and we are his;
  we are his people, and the sheep of his pasture.*
  Ps 100:1–2
- *My help comes from the LORD,
  who made heaven and earth.*
  Ps 121:2

Refuge

A very common way of speaking of God in the psalms is as refuge. This is a very comforting metaphor. God is the place to go when there is nowhere else to go. In past years I have also been compelled to pray with and for those we call refugees, those who are fleeing for safety and security, often from physical minefields, only to be caught in political minefields. The idea of refuge is linked with several other metaphors: rock, tent, shelter, fortress. Each person needs somewhere to go in time of trouble, somewhere safe and welcoming.

- *For he will hide me in his shelter*
  in the day of trouble;
  he will conceal me under the cover of his tent;
  he will set me high on a rock. Ps 27:5
- *In the shelter of your presence you hide them*
  from human plots;
  you hold them safe under your shelter
  from contentious tongues. Ps 31:20
- *God is our refuge and strength,*
  a very present help in trouble. Ps 46:1
- *You who live in the shelter of the Most High,*
  who abide in the shadow of the Almighty,
  will say to the LORD, 'My refuge and my fortress;
  my God, in whom I trust.' Ps 91:1–2

Shepherd

This familiar way of speaking of God comes from a social context that is very different from that of most city dwellers. Sheep and their shepherds were common sights in Israel. The interrelationship between shepherd and sheep was so familiar that it was used as a metaphor to speak of the king; and since God was the real king of Israel, it was also used to speak of the relationship between God and the people.

- *The LORD is my shepherd, I shall not want. Ps 23:1*
- *Then we your people, the flock of your pasture,*
  will give thanks to you for ever;
  from generation to generation
  we will recount your praise. Ps 79:13
- *Give ear, O Shepherd of Israel,*
  you who lead Joseph like a flock!
  You who are enthroned upon the cherubim,
  shine forth. Ps 80:1
- *For he is our God,*
  and we are the people of his pasture,
  and the sheep of his hand. Ps 95:7

Below: Shepherd with his flock in the Jordan Valley 1919, photograph (US public domain)

King David — the Patron of the Psalms

King David lived 3000 years ago and the Bible has many stories about him; often they are shaped by theological concerns rather than historical accuracy. The name of King David is in the superscription, or heading, of 73 psalms, mainly in books 1 and 2 of the Psalter. In the past this was understood to indicate that he was the composer of these psalms. Now most scholars understand the *l'david* superscription to indicate that the particular psalm belongs to a certain collection; it may also be a means of honouring the earlier King David and even a way of attributing a certain authority to the psalm by the use of his name in its superscription. Thus, he has become the patron of the psalms.

King David is known in the tradition for his musical skill. In 1 Sam 16 we read of him soothing King Saul with his harp. In 2 Sam 1 we hear that he composed a lament to mourn the death of King Saul and his son Jonathan. In 2 Sam 6 we have David accompanying the Ark of God as it was brought up to Jerusalem – he danced and made music in this procession.

Kingship was new to Israel in David's time (Saul, who precedes David, is the first king). Many were concerned that it was inappropriate for Israel to have an earthly king, as God was the true king of Israel. It was decided (as described in 1 Sam 8–12) that as long as the earthly king led the people in God's ways, the two kingships were not in conflict. However, history has shown that this alignment was not always the reality.

Below: King David, wooden sculpture in Church of our Lady, Breda, Netherlands

> **The significant dates for the Psalter**
>
> It seems that the growth of the book we call the Psalter was influenced by Israel's history. Some individual psalms use older language and belong in the time of the first Temple (900–587 BCE). Many scholars suggest that the final shape of the Psalter is post-Exilic – (after the return from Babylonian Exile in 537 BCE, and maybe even later). The Psalter was certainly used within the time of the second Temple (520 BCE–70 CE). Amidst the bewilderment of the apparent failure of God's covenant with David, we see the focus shift in the Psalter to the celebration of God as king. Thus, two kings and one city dominate the Psalter.

Zion, One City: City of David and City of God

David captured Jerusalem from the Jebusites (a Canaanite tribe – see Glossary) about 3000 years ago and made it the capital for the whole of Israel. His son Solomon also reigned from Jerusalem but after his death the kingdom was divided in two; from that time the city remained the capital of the smaller, southern kingdom, Judah. This city was known as 'the city of David' but it was also the city where the Temple was built by Solomon and in which God dwelt among the people.

The *Deuteronomistic History* (Deuteronomy, Joshua, Judges, Samuel and Kings) talks about God's name dwelling in the Temple as a way of speaking of God's immanent and intimate presence with the people. This city also became known as the city of God. The Zion psalms (Pss 46, 48, 84, 87, 122, 125, 128) honour God through prayer for and praise of this city and of all it represents. Naturally, when the psalmist speaks of the city, Jerusalem, Zion, he includes the inhabitants. Thus, two kings dominate the Psalter – King David, and the One he served: the supreme King of Israel and of all the earth.

The kingship of God is prominent in the last two books of the Psalter (Pss 90–150), while the name of David is more frequent in the first two books (Pss 1–72). Psalm 89 is at the end of the third book of the Psalter, and it laments the demise of the God's promise to David, the loss of a Davidic king on the throne of Judah, and indeed the loss of political independence for Judah.

Below: The Tower of David in the old city of Jerusalem, vintage watercolour

David is mentioned in seven psalms (Pss 18:50; 72:20; 78:70; 89:3, 20, 35, 49; 122:5; 132:10, 11, 17; 144:10). In several of these, David is spoken of as God's *messiah*. This term means 'anointed' – within the biblical tradition it comes to mean 'God's anointed'. Prophets and kings were anointed as a sign of their being commissioned by God for a task which promoted God's plans for Israel. David was a *messiah* and entered into the Davidic covenant (2 Sam 7) which was expected to last forever.

David in the Psalms

In the earlier section on Genre, we saw that Psalm 51 is one of the psalms which is linked to an event in David's life. It fits well with the general theme of the penitential lament, but there is nothing specific in the text of the psalm to suggest adultery or murder, which were the sins of David. It is the same with the other psalms with an historical link to David in their superscription; the psalm has a theme which fits with the events in David's life but few specifics which really tie the psalm with David. These links with David's life make the psalm real: it belongs in real-life contexts, and invites readers to use their imagination as to other real-life contexts where this psalm could be prayed.

David's name abounds in the Psalter and he remains a central figure there. His role is not so much one of authorship as one of theological significance and this may well be far more important. There are psalms which are clearly much later than David: Psalm 137 and Psalm 74 are written after the experience of the Babylonian exile; several psalms mention the Temple or God's house or the place where God's name dwells: these presuppose the Temple has been built which was after David died. There are also psalms where the language is late Hebrew and which therefore could not have been written by David.

No one can tell us if David wrote any of the psalms but we do know that his name is very deliberately linked with the psalms. He cannot be named the author of any specific psalm but he is the patron who lent his authority to the psalms. For these reasons they are known as the psalms of David.

Psalm 110
Of David. A Psalm.

This psalm has a simple superscription: *l'david. Mizmor*, meaning 'Of David. A Psalm'. The brevity of the superscription leaves many details unknown. The remainder of the text does not mention David and it does not even specify a king – but implies one. The text mentions a priest *according to the order of Melchizedek*. This name is derived from *melech*/king and *zedek*/righteousness; thus, the king of righteousness. This psalm probably originated in the time of actual kings in Judah (1000–587 BCE) and seems to contain certain propaganda for the reigning king: he has God's support so who could be against him?

Verse 1 is better understood as an oracle of the LORD. The word 'oracle' is used almost exclusively in relation to God's utterances and especially in the prophetic literature. The text has God speak directly and offers the king a seat of honour. The prophetic nuance gives the psalm added authority. The earthly lord (the king?) is invited to the seat at the right hand of the heavenly LORD, a place of honour and prestige, while his enemies are to be subjected to humiliation in his presence.

In verse 2 we see that it is from Zion that God sends out the sceptre of the king and this suggests that a Davidic king is the intended object of the oracle. Then a second oracle is uttered by God in verse 4, which also honours the king. There are textual difficulties in this psalm and so it is not always clear exactly what is intended but this royal psalm honours and supports the earthly king, who is also priest. The oracle, with its prophetic overtones, suggests that the king has God's approval and support. In this sense this is an appropriate psalm to pray for our national leaders today. Through this psalm we pray that our political leaders will be righteous and thereby be honoured by God.

Early Christians, as we see in the New Testament, came to understand this psalm in relation to Jesus as priest, prophet and king, their righteous teacher, who they believed was honoured by God in his resurrection.

The Structure of Psalm 110

Verses 1–3
Words to the king
by God and their realisation.

Verses 4–7
Words to the king
by God and their realisation.

We see that the pattern
is repeated,
thus adding emphasis.

Background: reconstruction of second temple

1000 BCE	King David
950 BCE	First Temple – King Solomon
922 BCE	Two Kingdoms – Israel and Judah
722 BCE	Israel defeated and disappears as a political reality
597 BCE	Babylonian Exile begins
587 BCE	Second stage of Babylonian exile – Temple in Jerusalem destroyed
537 BCE	Return from Babylon
520 BCE	Second Temple built in Jerusalem
70 CE	Second Temple destroyed by Romans
	Rise of Rabbinic Judaism and Christianity

Jesus Prayed the Psalms

We do not have any detailed information about Jesus praying the psalms, but we do know that he was an observant Jew, so he would have known and prayed the psalms both personally and with his people in synagogue and temple.

Jesus was both human and divine. His humanity was within a specific people, at a specific time in history, in a particular land and culture. He spoke the language of his people, and worshipped God according to their customs. Jesus was born into a Jewish family and Mary his mother was Jewish as was Joseph. He came to know God as YHWH/LORD within his tradition and worshipped God in the forms of first century Judaism.

The Judaism of his time was diverse, with several factions which thought differently about the Scriptures and worship, and politics – much like Christians of today. Jesus was never a Christian, and his baptism by John was not Christian baptism. In his adult life, most of his followers were also Jews; even the evangelists, when writing his story many years after his death, looked to the Scriptures known to Jews for the meaning of Jesus' life.

We can picture him as a Jewish child learning the psalms within his family, praying them personally, in his local synagogue in Nazareth and in the temple in Jerusalem, especially during the major feasts. We do not have direct evidence of this, but through our knowledge of Judaism in the time of Jesus we can deduce that it was so.

Above and below (detail): Joseph teaching Jesus scripture, bronze by Pauline Clayton, St Francis Church, Melbourne

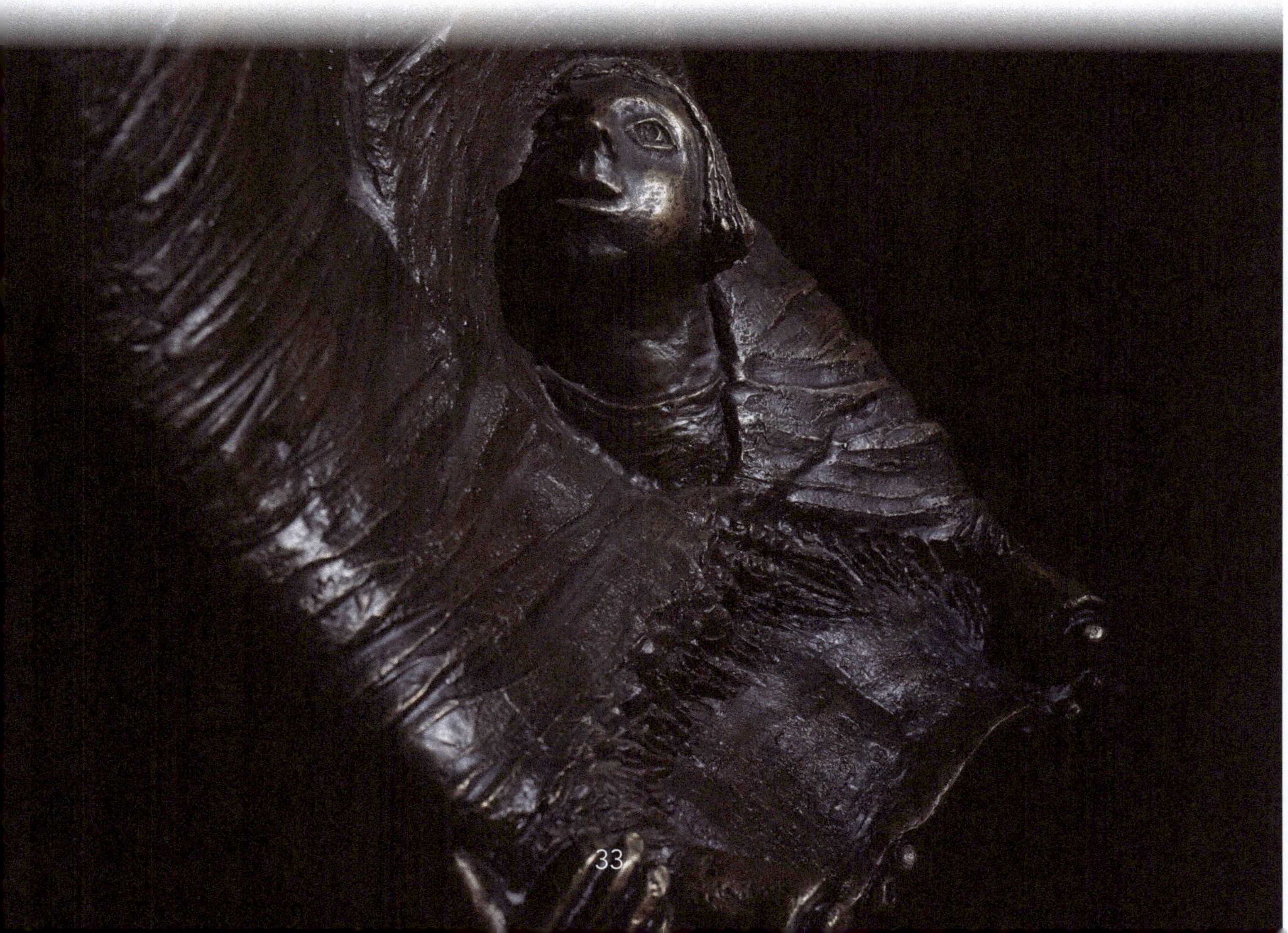

Above: Jesus: 6th century icon from St Katherine's Monastery, Mt Sinai. This is one of the oldest images of Jesus

Below: The Golden Gate to the old city of Jerusalem

Opposite page: gazelles

The Psalms in the Gospels

We do know that the four Evangelists all placed psalm texts on the lips of Jesus.

Matthew has Jesus quote Psalms 110, 22, 8, 118 (Mt 22:44; Mt 27:46; Mt 21:16; Mt 21:42 & 23:39). **Mark** has Jesus quote the same psalms and **Luke** likewise but he adds Psalm 31 in Lk 23:46. **John's** Gospel adds Psalms 35, 69, 41, 78, 82 (John 15:25 & John 2:17 & John 19:28-29; John 13:18; John 6:31; John 10:34). Therefore, the Evangelists not only have Jesus speak the words of psalms but also looked to the psalms to explain the meaning of Jesus to their particular communities.

Two of the Synoptic Gospels, in telling the story of the Last Supper, say: *and when they had sung a hymn they went out to the Mount of Olives.* (Mt 26:30; Mk 14:26) this is surely a reference to the Jewish practice of reciting the Hallel psalms (113–118) throughout the Passover meal and at its conclusion. For that reason the Gospels suggest that Jesus and his disciples were following this custom for Passover when Jesus was about to enter into his passion.

We are told in Luke's Gospel that the family took Jesus as a boy to the Temple in Jerusalem. Luke 2:41-42 suggests it was the family's custom to go to Jerusalem for the feasts or at least for the feast of Passover: *Now every year his parents went to Jerusalem for the festival of the Passover. And when he was twelve years old, they went up as usual for the festival.*

There were three pilgrim feasts, Passover/Pesach, Pentecost/Shavuot and Tabernacles/Succoth and Jewish men who could do so were required to go up to the Temple in Jerusalem for these feasts. The liturgical celebrations for these feasts were replete with psalms. Psalms 120–134 are headed 'Psalms of Ascent' and many scholars suggest that these were prayed by the pilgrims en route to Jerusalem for the feasts and more specifically as they began the long ascent to Jerusalem. As mentioned above, the Hallel psalms 113–118 and the Great Hallel Psalm 136 were associated with the main feasts in Temple times, and in a special way with the feast of Passover.

Jesus went up to Jerusalem

Because of its geography, a traveller literally has to 'go up' to Jerusalem, especially from the west and from the east. This geographical reality has

taken on a theological dimension. Metaphorically, God was understood to be 'up there' and so in biblical narratives one 'goes up' to encounter God. In several texts, God's name, or God's presence, is spoken of as residing in the Temple in Jerusalem. And so, for the feasts, when a pilgrim 'goes up' to Jerusalem, to the Temple, it is understood that the person will encounter God, in the city of God.

The concept of the 'heavenly' Jerusalem is closely linked to the 'earthly' Jerusalem, but is projected into the future and beyond the Earth. Both were understood as the place of meeting with God. The time and geographical references change.

In going up to Jerusalem as a boy, and later as an adult, Jesus would have prayed the psalms with his people. When he arrived at the Temple he would have offered *a sacrifice of praise* (Heb 13:15 & Ps 50:14), also using the words of the psalms.

Psalms as prophecy

In a very different way, our Christian interpretations have read the psalms as prophecy. This presupposes a foretelling in the psalms. It is one way to understand prophecy but certainly not the only understanding of it. This prophetic lens is evident in some of the New Testament quotes of psalms. Consequently, David was thought by the evangelists to be foretelling the events in Jesus' life. Thus, Jesus is portrayed in Acts as:

*the stone that was rejected by you, the builders;
it has become the cornerstone.*

(quoting psalm 118)
There is salvation in no one else, for there is no other name under heaven given among mortals by which we must be saved. Acts 4:10–12

Acts takes a verse from Ps 118 and applies it to Jesus. This application comes from a belief that everything in the Scripture speaks about Jesus. We do need to be careful how we use this method of interpretation as it comes from our faith in Jesus – but it does not mean that the original author was speaking about Jesus when writing the text. I believe that the early Christian community, especially the Evangelists, used familiar texts, especially psalm texts, to express the meaning of Jesus for their community and to use the authority of their biblical tradition to enhance their words.

We have seen how David was named *messiah* in several psalms. This title is later applied to Jesus, who is of the family and line of David and inheritor of God's promise that someone of David's line will continue his rule. Christians understand this covenant with David as continued in Jesus. The covenant with David suggests that there will always be a descendant of David on the throne of Judah.

This theological tradition was later given an eschatological significance in the Jewish community before Jesus' time. They tried to make sense of God's promise to David, which, because there was no longer a Davidic king, seemed to have been abandoned. This would indicate that God had not been true to God's word and that could not be imagined. Thus developed a concept of *messiah* which took on a future, and sometimes eschatological, orientation.

Psalm 22
To the leader: according to The Deer of the Dawn. A Psalm of David.

This is a lament of an individual. It was written many years before the time of Jesus. Some of its verses are placed by the Evangelists on the lips of Jesus as he dies upon the cross. In

The Structure of Psalm 22

Main Sections

Verses 1–21a
The troubles
of the speaker.

Verses 21b–31
Thanks for the assured or actual
resolution of the problem.

Detailed Structure
Verse 1

Note the intimacy here. The psalmist has a long relationship with God and knows it is founded in the story of his people. The pronoun itself indicates this, *My God*, not God. It is unusual to feel abandoned by a stranger, it is the one closest we need beside us in times of severe trouble and pain. It is a beloved whose apparent abandonment is felt keenly. The why occurs only once in the Hebrew but is understood for each part/cola of the verse. Why abandoned?
Why distant? Why not listening?

Verses 2–5
Contrasts between the psalmist and God and
between how God acted in the past
and the psalmist's present.

Verses 6–8
Psalmist debased by
self and ridiculed by others

Verses 9–10
God's care of the psalmist at birth – in the past

Verse 11
Plea for help in the present

Verses 12–18
Emotive descriptions of the present suffering

Verses 19–21
Plea for help in the present

Verses 22–31
Promise of praise in the future

---

its origins it was not written about him but was used by the followers of Jesus, mainly Jews, to speak about him and the meaning and intensity of his suffering.

By citing the tradition, and understanding David as speaking about Jesus prophetically, they ensured that Jesus was portrayed as the awaited *messiah*. The quoting of Scripture and the claim that David foretold him lent authority to the claims of the followers of the Way about Jesus. It is important to remember that this psalm pre-dates the historical Jesus and to take time to ponder the text before praying it with Jesus.

Past, Present and Future as a Continuum

It is in the present that the psalmist suffers, and the suffering is physical, emotional, spiritual and psychological. Forsaken (v 1), dehumanised (vv 6–7), surrounded by forces of oppression and evil (vv 12–13), depleted (v 14), silenced (v 15), overwhelmed (v 16), and stripped (v 18).

Yet there are verses where the psalmist remembers the past, the early experience of intimacy at the moment of birth. Birth in biblical times was a time of great vulnerability for both mother and child. The psalmist remembers not only that God was present at the time of his birth but was active and is portrayed as midwife (vv 9–10), assisting in the birthing and in placing him on the mother's breast, the place of nurture and security for a newborn child. This personal experience of God's action for life for the psalmist interplays with the earlier verses, again referring to the past, where God was trusted by the ancestors and they were not shamed: God delivered them.

The final third of the psalm has two sections of praise: vv 22–26 & 27–31. It looks to the future: *I will tell of your name ...* The first section focuses on praise with the congregation, probably in the Temple in Jerusalem. The second section looks to all the ends of the earth as they acknowledge God's power and kingship. Thus, the future, when praise is possible, is a time when things will have been transformed and everyone, all nations, can proclaim deliverance because of God's action, saying: *He has done it.*

Past, present and future are portrayed as a continuum, and the past sustains the psalmist in the painful present as he has confidence in a transformed future.

Psalm 22 from the cross

This psalm is placed on the lips of Jesus as he dies upon the cross. *My God, my God, why have you forsaken me*, by Matthew (27:46) and by Mark (15:34). The opening verse of the psalm puts before us a suggestion that the physical suffering of Jesus was less intense than the sense of being abandoned by God, his father. This does not imply despair, as shown by the simple fact that it is addressed to God, *my God*. However, it does indicate how severe was the pain and the sense of abandonment for Jesus, and how intense this can be for us when we too feel abandoned by God. It contains an invitation to pray this psalm with and for people in desperate situations: war, pandemic, extreme drought, fires, political oppression, economic hopelessness, and terminal illness.

Some scholars like to imagine that the Evangelists implied the whole psalm when quoting the opening line. I think this is because the last ten verses are a promise of praise, in the future. However, it is not necessary to imply the whole psalm so as to avoid a suggestion of despair, for as mentioned above, the opening invocation *My God* has already told us that the Evangelists did not intend despair. The invitation is to pray this psalm with Jesus in his suffering and with all today who suffer in similar ways.

Jesus prayed the psalms as a Jewish man in Galilee and in Jerusalem. The Evangelists chose words from the psalms to give expression to his emotions, especially during his passion and death. Today's invitation is to pray the psalms with Jesus in our day and in light of our experiences.

There are other references to this psalm in the Gospels

Ps 22:18
They divide my clothes among themselves, and for my clothing they cast lots. Jn 19:23–24; Mt 27:35; Mk 15:24; Lk 23:34

Ps 22:7
All who see me mock at me; they make mouths at me, they shake their heads: Mt 27:39; Mk 15:29

Ps 22:8
Commit your cause to the Lord; let him deliver – let him rescue the one in whom he delights! Mt 27:43

Ps 22:31
Saying that he has done it. Jn 19:30

Below: Psalm 22 gives voice to intense suffering, including the feeling of being abandoned by God and yet it hopes for a future beyond the suffering. We can use this psalm when we feel abandoned.

Hebrew Poetry

We have focused a good deal on the religious nature of the psalms. It is important to also examine their literary nature. They are written texts that are literature; in particular they are poetry – Hebrew poetry. Poetry engages our experience, our emotions and our senses through words.

Samuel Taylor Coleridge has described poetry as 'the best words in the best order'. Yet in the psalms we are dealing with a translation and therefore we lose the order and some of the succinctness of the text. However, even in translation we can find the beauty and allure of this literature.

Some of the characteristics of Hebrew poetry are: succinctness, imagery, metaphor and a tendency to repeat the idea, in what is called *parallelism*. Another way in which psalmic poetry conveys meaning is by alluding to other biblical texts within and beyond the psalter, and therefore expanding and deepening the text by bringing it into a network of meaning.

Poetry touches emotions but it also requires some intellectual attention to appreciate its specific techniques. An emotional response is often immediate and unmediated, while a deepened encounter requires attention and analysis. Both are important and fruitful.

Parallelism

Psalm 103
Of David

This is the most unexpected characteristic of Biblical poetry. It appears to be repetition, but it is far more. An example from Psalm 103 will allow us to examine parallelism.

> a. Bless the LORD, O my soul,
> b. and all that is within me, bless his holy name. Ps 103:1

At first reading this verse says the same thing twice. However, it is more than simple repetition, the second half of the verse is more particular and spells out aspects of the meaning of the first line.

The first colon (each part of the verse is called a *colon*; most verses are *bicola* and some longer and *tricola*) is a simple call to self to bless the Lord; the second half is inviting not merely myself but *all that is within me* to bless God. The psalmist speaks to his *nephesh*, soul, which is the inner being, the essence of the person and exhorts the self to bless the LORD/YHWH. The poet has called upon himself to bless God's holy name and then has made sure we understand that *self* equates to *all that is within me*.

The object of this verse is the LORD and the second colon particularises: it is the holiness of God's name which is to be honoured. The first instance uses the sacred name YHWH (which is sensitively translated as LORD in capital letters in the NRSV). In the second colon it does not use the sacred name but spells out that it is the holiness of that name which the cause of this impulse.

Parallelism has allowed the pray-er to absorb the general sense conveyed by both cola and also, with attention and study, it reveals the specificity of meaning. Experienced teachers know the importance of repetition; the psalmist here finds a way to retain the emphasis by repetition and to add an extra dimension for those willing to stop and reflect on the text.

Parallelism works at several levels in many psalms. A straightforward example is in Ps 103:13: *As a father has compassion for his children, so the LORD has compassion for all those who fear him* (hold God in awe). It moves from a familiar experience, the compassion of fathers, to a theological statement about God.

Verses 15–17 are a more developed use of parallelism. The comparison develops from a simple statement about the shortness of human life (in v 15) to a reminder that in time we will not be

remembered (in v 16) to a contrast (in v 17) where God's everlasting nature is introduced by reference to *hesed*, which is offered eternally. Thus, the simple parallelism is expanded to highlight the reliability and everlasting nature of God in contrast to the fleeting lives of mortals.

Contrasting Parallelism

There is another form of parallelism found in Hebrew poetry: *contrasting* parallelism. In these instances, there is a contrast between the first half of the verse and the second half, rather than a sense of repetition and intensification.

Psalm 1:6
Two Ways

There is not an example of this in Psalm 103, so I will return to Ps 1:6 to give an example.

> *... for the Lord watches over the way of the righteous,*
> *but the way of the wicked will perish.*

Psalm 1, which confronts the reader with the choice about what sort of person they wish to be, concludes with this verse and, using contrasting or antithetic parallelism, highlights the consequence of the choice. Do you want the LORD to watch over your path in life, or do you wish to follow a path that leads nowhere, that perishes? It is important to note that the text does not say that the wicked perish, but that their path, or way, perishes. Thus Ps 1:6 concludes with a contrast which invites a decision, even a commitment.

Images

A simile describes something as being 'like' something else, whereas a metaphor transfers meaning from something familiar to something unknown or unexpected. It conveys meaning about one thing through either a likeness or dissimilarity to something unrelated. This is important if we are to speak about God, who is essentially *other*, in ways that can be communicated and understood. Metaphors allow

us to speak of intangible things like love, pain, and even God, in ways which are intelligible to others. They provide an insight into the meaning being conveyed but they are not a definition. If I describe God as a *shepherd* I am not being exact or saying all there is to say about God. But the more I know about shepherds the more this metaphor conveys about God. It is important to note that I need to understand shepherds in biblical times, which is quite different from a shepherd in the Australian outback.

Israel banned images in worship, in case the image itself was worshipped instead of God, but in its literature it could not do away with images. In the psalms, images abound. In all of Israel's poetry we find diverse images, while in its worship the ban on visual images continued. The verbal images were essential in order to speak of God, of strong emotions and of intangible truths. The images used were usually commonplace and familiar, but the ways they were applied was sometimes unusual.

Earlier, the metaphor of midwife was examined. Who would have thought of this term to describe God? Yet it conveys the life-centred nature of God, the creator, and at the same time the intimate and personal nature of the relationship between a human being and God. The midwife receives the newborn at a moment of danger and vulnerability which is also a time of wondrous possibility. This metaphor suggests that God facilitates human life in the most personal and tender ways.

Succinctness

Poets tend to choose their words carefully and use them sparsely. Israel's poets often omitted words felt to be unnecessary; they used prefixes and suffixes to lessen the number of words in a verse. As we saw earlier, they often allowed a word to be stated in a colon and merely understood in the second colon without being repeated.

We lose a great deal of the succinctness in translation and yet, when compared with prose texts, we can still see that the poetry of the psalms is brief. What might this brevity contribute? Because of the economy of details given by the text we, the readers, need to bring our experience and imagination to the reception of the text.

Few words, many gaps, images and emotions: these elements of poetry invite me into the world of the psalmist and at the same time require me to touch my own experience in order to fathom the meaning. The words from the past resonate with the present of the reader, and in this process we make meaning.

Rhythm

There is rhythm in Hebrew poetry but it is not as consistent as some poets would like. Translation works against the retention of rhythm. Yet it remains in the original.

Structure

There are several ways of looking at the movement within a psalm. The associated structures are sometimes

Below: Palestinian shepherd, photo from 'Pilgrimage to Palestine' by Yuvachyov, before 1904 (US public domain)

> **The Structure of Psalm 77**
>
> **Main divisions**
> Verses 1–10
> Lament
>
> Verses 11–20
> Hymnic
>
> **Detailed Structure**
> Verses 1–2
> Cry to God
>
> Verses 3–6
> Deep Lament
>
> Verses 7–9
> The Psalmist Questions
>
> Verses 10–15
> The Past Remembered Verses
>
> Verses 16–20
> The Past Celebrated.

indicated by the text itself and at other times discerned by the reader. In the latter instances there may be more than one way to understand the flow and associated structure. Scholars often differ in this regard and you may change your mind over time. There can be more than one way to see the structure and associated movement within a psalm. Working to discover the structure helps the reader attend to what is happening as the psalm reveals its meaning.

Sometimes the repetition of words indicates movement within a psalm. Psalm 77 indicates this through the use of pronouns. In verses 1–7 first person singular abounds: *I, me, my*. Then in verses 8–11 the third person singular is dominant: *he, his*. In verse 12 another change takes place and the second person singular is introduced: *you* and *your*. This usage highlights the change taking place within the psalmist and the one praying. Brueggemann has called this 'The turn from self to God'. It is the psalm itself which portrays the change through the way it uses pronouns. The psalmist begins with a certain fixation of self and then addresses God in the third person before the final movement to second person *you*. This recognises the importance of maintaining a focus on self until the pain is expunged and the one praying is able to recognise the presence of the other and finally to enter into an I-THOU relationship.

In a similar way Psalm 103 indicates a movement from the individual, to Israel, to all humanity and to the whole created order and then returns to the individual.

INTERPLAY WITH OTHER BIBLICAL TEXTS

Psalm 103 alludes to a text which is extremely well known in Jewish

> *The LORD is merciful and gracious,*
> *slow to anger and abounding in steadfast love.*
> *He will not always accuse,*
> *nor will he keep his anger forever.*
> *He does not deal with us according to our sins,*
> *nor repay us according to our iniquities.*
> Ps 103:8–10

> *The LORD, the LORD, a God merciful and gracious,*
> *slow to anger, and abounding in steadfast love and faithfulness,*
> *keeping steadfast love for the thousandth generation,*
> *forgiving iniquity and transgression and sin,*
> *yet by no means clearing the guilty,*
> *but visiting the iniquity of the parents upon the children*
> *and the children's children,*
> *to the third and the fourth generation.*
> Ex 34:6–7

tradition but not so familiar to Christians. In verses 8–10 it is almost quoting Ex 34:6–7 and thus would have brought to the mind of the readers close to the time of the original community and many Jewish readers of today the wonderful description of God in this Exodus text.

The Poetry of the Psalms in Psalm 103

In itself this is a most beautiful hymn, which takes us on an expanding sense of community. It begins with the psalmist talking to self. We know from experience the importance of these conversations, when there is no one to overhear our words, and we can be honest and spontaneous. The individual speaks about the desire to bless God and to remember, not forget, all the good things received in life: forgiveness, healing, renewal and having days filled with good things. The remembering then broadens to proclaim the goodness and salvation Israel has experienced.

This is followed by an even wider audience, all mortals. All have been the recipients of the blessings of compassion and *hesed*. The psalm ends with a call to angels, and all hosts, possibly stars, to join in a cosmic hymn of praise to the reliable and everlasting God, who as creator is in a covenantal relationship with all that has been created. The concentric circles are the expanding of community with whom the individual offers praise and to some extent thanks. This is our call today, to expand our sense of community to include not only all mortals but also animals, plants, planets and stars.

This psalm has shown us how the various aspects of Hebrew poetry unite to invite us to respond to goodness and to God.

Community Prayer

Prayer is an expression of an intimate and developing relationship with God, allowing God's presence to influence our ways of being and acting. The psalms, many of which are prayers, remind us that the relationship with God is based in truth and life and they give voice to this. They are based in truth in that they express a great range of emotions: joy, need, desire ... They are based in life in that they arise from the human experiences from the past. St Athanasius said that a psalm 'is a mirror in which you contemplate yourself and the movements of your soul'. The psalms take us inwards, to the depth of our own being and call us out to the community, to the world and especially to those who suffer.

Our Common Voice

Giving voice through the words of the psalms to our emotions and experience, is usually a means of growth in the spiritual life. Raw and honest communication with the Beloved can change us, help us to become more aware of who we are and what we really want. Psalm 42–43 articulates a deep longing and thereby is an excellent example to explore in this chapter. Its questions open up several dialogues: with God, with self and with enemies.

We are all called to see ourselves as part of humanity and indeed as within the whole community of life, including animals and plants. The very last verse of the psalter calls us to join with everything that breathes in praising the Lord.

In the development of our spiritual life and its nurturance, the psalms help us to be honest with God, to allow a community of believers to grow together through their shared life and prayer and to reach beyond those who are familiar to embrace all humans and the whole web of life.

Our spiritual life does not develop in isolation. We link with traditions, with other people, with the created order and with our own heart and experience as we grow spiritually. Hermits and members of enclosed orders do not pray alone. They pray with others beyond their ken and their own experience. They pray for all who have found a place in their heart and I do not simply mean that they pray for others but that they pray with others, with a much wider community than those they can actually see. They pray with those facing war, famine and disease; those who are ignored and forgotten; those who rejoice in new life and old age, and those who are quietly grateful for a moment of beauty.

Earlier we have discussed various ways that psalms assist personal prayer. Here we will focus on some communal prayer forms in which psalms are prayed together. They become our common voice.

Responsorial Psalms

The place where most Christians will collectively pray a psalm is in churches, as a response to a reading from Scripture. In the Catholic tradition this is called the Responsorial Psalm. Many do not pay a great deal of attention to this psalm, yet it carries the message of the other readings, especially the first reading, and gives us a common response. Ideally the response is chanted or sung. This provides the community with a collective response to God's word and the nourishment it offers.

We can pray together through the response or refrain, usually a verse from the psalm, and so the psalm

facilitates a communal dialogue with God. The refrain can remain with us as we go into the world to live what we have celebrated; with the energy and nourishment we have received. And because we have sung the refrain a few times it stays with us even as we go to live our humdrum and extraordinary lives.

My disappointment is that often the psalm text is incomplete because only a section of the psalm is used for the Responsorial Psalm. I encourage everyone to read the whole psalm either in preparation for or follow-up to the community worship.

An example in relation to Psalm 42–43 may throw light on the importance of the Responsorial Psalm. In Catholic tradition it is used for the Responsorial Psalm during the Easter Vigil, after Reading 7 (Ezekiel 36:16–28) (the Vigil can have 9 readings before the Gospel).

To be precise: verses 3–5 of Psalm 42 and verse 3–4 of Psalm 43 are used.

We explore later the continuance of Psalm 42 in Psalm 43. It begins with the very familiar words: *As a deer longs for flowing streams, so my soul longs for you, O God.*

These become the words of the refrain. They are the words which we sing four times as a response to the Ezekiel text where God promises to bring the people of Israel home from Exile, to cleanse them, give them a new heart and put a new spirit within them.

Christians hear these words addressed to them during the Easter Vigil and respond in the words of Psalm 42–43. The longing articulated in the psalm becomes the longing of the Christian community as it awaits the Resurrection during the Vigil service.

This is a beautiful example of how the Responsorial Psalm gives us a common response to a common emotion as we hold our breath in anticipation of the Risen One.

Prayer of the Church (Liturgy of the Hours, Divine Office)

This prayer, the Liturgy of the Hours, has several forms and several names. In the Catholic tradition the Mass, together with the Divine Office, constitute the official public prayer of the Church. The aim of the Liturgy of the Hours is to mark the hours of the day with prayer, especially the turning points of the day.

It is comprised of:
- The Office of Readings
- Matins (during the night)
- Lauds (dawn)
- Prime (early morning)
- Terce (mid-morning)
- Sext (midday)
- None (mid-afternoon)
- Vespers (evening) and
- Compline (night).

Below: German nuns singing the psalms by Claus Meyer (1856–1919)

Traditionally these arose in monasteries and almost simultaneously in cathedrals. It was a continuation of a Jewish practice of reciting prayers at certain times throughout the day, based on texts like Ps 55:17. The form in cathedrals was the clergy with the people, not necessarily the same people for each part of the day, but it was the prayer of the local community.

In monasteries it was usually the monks or nuns of the community who saw this as their role for the whole of the church. Today many people have taken to praying one or more of these Hours each day – some in their parish or in a small group, some individually, and always with the whole world.

While many priests and clergy are obliged to recite all of these Hours, there is a form of this prayer which invites us all to mark even the beginning and end of the day with Lauds and Vespers or Compline. In earlier times, the cathedral form was the prayer of the local community. It seems to me that it is time to reclaim this tradition in our parishes.

Through this regular praying of all the different psalms and their varying genres, the psalms become familiar. When a lament is presented, the psalms offer an opportunity to pray with those who suffer; when a thanksgiving psalm is offered, we can pray with those who offer heartfelt gratitude; and when a hymn is raised to God, it is for those who delight in all things great and small.

Thus, the psalms help us to expand our hearts as we pray the Liturgy of the Hours. We expand our day with moments of prayer and we sensitise our hearts as we experience the emotions represented in the psalms and become ever more aware of those experiencing these deep emotions around us and throughout the world. This practice, especially via the psalms, opens our being to God and to all of our sisters and brothers.

Why mention the Liturgy of the Hours in *A Friendly Guide to the Book of Psalms*? The bulk of the Liturgy of the Hours is psalms. The usual structure is an opening response and prayer, followed by a short reading from Scripture, three psalms, intercessions and concluding with another short prayer. This varies a little, but you can see how central the psalms are to the structure: the idea is that over a set time, (usually four weeks) all, or nearly all, the psalms will be prayed. This takes away the selective possibilities; we pray them all, because we know that somewhere, some humans are experiencing the emotions expressed in the particular psalms even as we pray them.

We also suspect that at different times in our own lives we have experienced these same emotions and desires.

Below: Choir of holy women by Josef Kastner in Carmelite church, Döbling, Vienna, 19th century

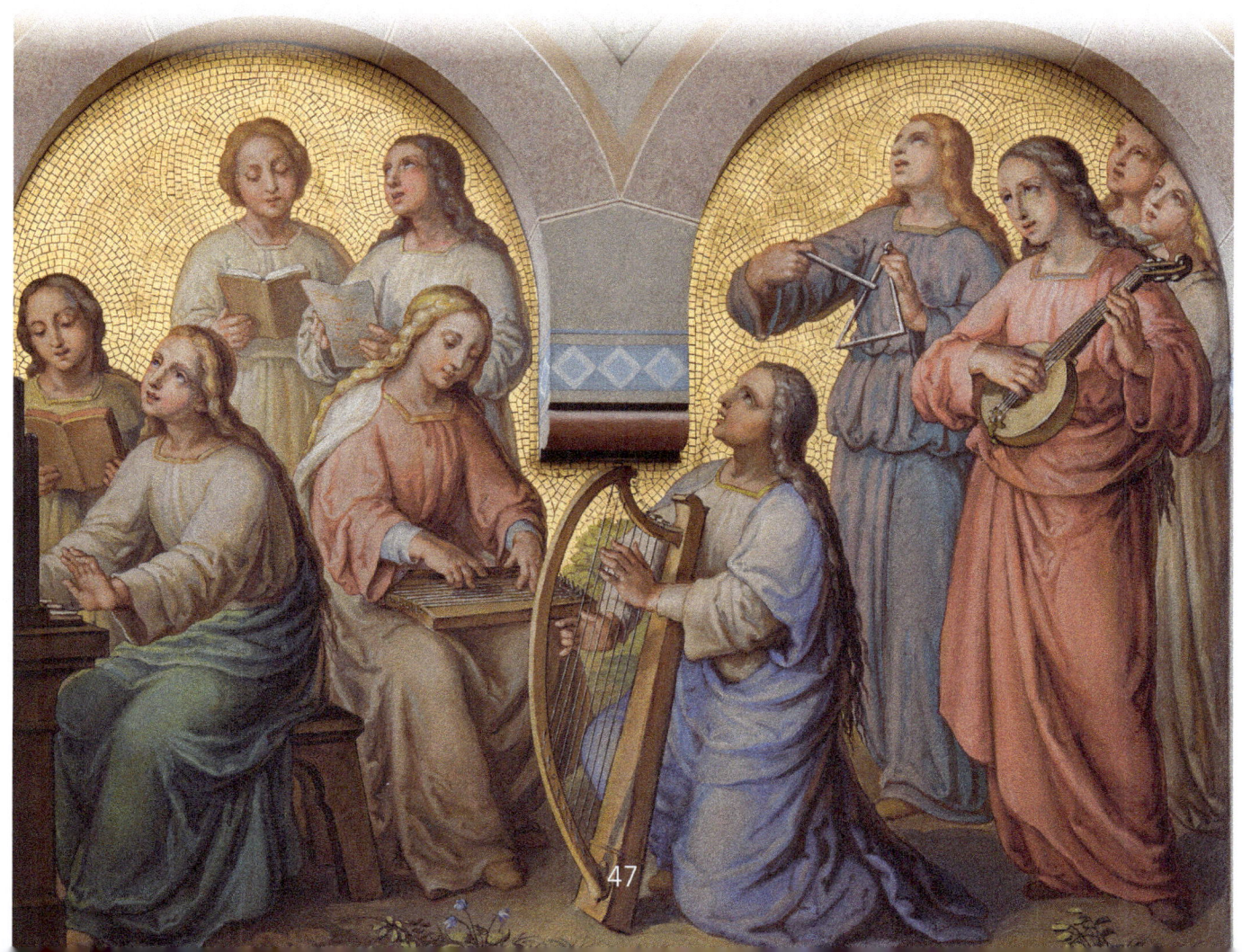

Lectio Divina

This literally means a divine reading of the text, a sacred reading, a holy reading. It requires a safe and quiet place, an open bible and maybe a candle or flower. Nothing cluttered, nothing hurried. It is an experience of silence and listening; an experience of stillness; an encounter with God, through the Scripture, the psalm text. It asks you to be gentle with yourself and to enter into this time expecting blessings and graces. Remember that God's revelation continues through God's word today and to you.

This is a simple and profound method of praying the Scriptures and especially the psalms. It can be used individually or by a group. The roots of *Lectio Divina* are in the story of St Benedict (480–547) but it was formalised a few centuries later. Recently Cardinal Carlo Maria Martini, of Milan (1980–2002), offered this form of prayer to his people and soon they were filling the Cathedral to be nourished by God's word.

The **Lectio** step is facilitated by reading the text aloud two or three times. What do you notice? What are the main images you see in this psalm? What is the feel of this psalm? What genre is it? What is the movement from beginning to end? You may note the context in the literature: is it the last psalm in the Psalter or paired with its neighbouring psalm or a *Halleluyah* psalm or …? Does this link enhance its meaning?

This step is named *Lectio*, or reading, however, it does not mean a cursory reading. It entails several readings and often some wider reading about the text. Some people skip over the profound possibilities of this first step, to their loss.

This stage may include reading a commentary on this particular psalm. It highlights the depth to which reading or *Lectio* may take us. This is based in a belief that the Scripture, in this case the psalm text, is the Word of God and thereby worthy of close attention so that we do not fail to really heed the text. It is important that we listen and not make it say what we want to hear. It is grounded in a deep listening to the text at hand. Many find that a verse or phrase becomes their focus, in a sense the verse has chosen you. Through this choice, this attraction, God addresses your present reality or need.

The **Meditatio** step is focused on the spiritual link between the text and you, the individual, and your life and experience. Allow your life to interact with this text. What is the meaning of this text for you? What does it tell you about yourself and God?

Below: Saint Benedict, statue in Piazza San Benedetto, Norcia, Italy

To what does it invite you? What messages within the psalm are you called to integrate into your life? This is a reflective stage, a time to attend to your response to the psalm text, to God. Words are few, attention is essential.

The **Oratio** step is you talking to God in response to the text, to God's word to you. There are no rules. You do not have to talk nicely to God. Your prayer needs to be honest and can be emotional. In prayer you seek the grace you desire as a response to your *Lectio* and *Meditatio*.

Contemplatio is stillness; you wait in silence and allow God to respond. There is no guarantee of an answer but we are shaped by a sense of God's presence or even absence. Receptivity is characteristic of this step.

Operatio is what happens as we go forth to live our lives. This is not the assured result of one experience of *Lectio Divina* but the cumulative grace of allowing God's word to address us. It may be a word we take which reminds us of what we desire, or an action, a commitment.

Lectio Divina has been described above as it may be used by an individual. Yet it is equally a method for a group to use in common prayer. The more comfortable the group members are with each other the richer will be the sharing which arises in the use of *Lectio Divina*.

Lectio Divina

1. *Lectio* – Reading –
What am I reading?

2. *Meditatio* – Meditation –
What does this evoke in my relationship with God?

3. *Oratio* – Prayer –
What do I wish to say to God?

4. *Contemplatio* –
Contemplation – listen, wait, allow God space.

5. *Operatio* –
Application to life. Go and act from this time of prayer.

PSALM 42 – 43
To the Leader. A Maskil of the Korahites.

This is a lament, in the singular, which gives voice to the pain of separation. The separation from God, as the opening verse conveys, and separation from the community as verse four suggests. Some scholars believe that the Babylonian Exile is the background and this could be so but there is little evidence to allow such specificity.

The common elements of the lament genre are only clear when continuing into Psalm 43. The pain is tangible in Psalm 42 and the prayer and promise are only found in Psalm 43. The common refrain also highlights the unity of the psalm. One less obvious detail confirms the unity; these psalms are within a group of Korahite psalms (Pss 42–49) but Psalm 43 does not mention Korah in the superscription, in fact it does not even have a superscription, as do all the other psalms in this collection. This is the final evidence to confirm that Psalm 43 is a continuation of Psalm 42.

The longing to be with God and with the worshipping community is captured especially in the questions: *When shall I come and behold the face of God? Where is your God? Why are you cast down, O my soul, and why are you disquieted within me? Why have you forgotten me? Why must I walk about mournfully because the enemy oppresses me? Why have you cast me off?*

Only one question points to an external cause of the isolation, enemies, and their question is within the refrain: '*Where is your God?*'. Thus, both the psalmist and the enemies see the cause of the problem in the same way. The implication is that God's absence is the issue. The enemies see this as a reason to jeer and imply the absence is due to powerlessness on the part of Israel's God. The psalmist, however, knows that this will change and that the solution is to hope in God and thus the psalmist repeats the refrain three times. The other witness to the depth of hope by the psalmist is the promise that when (not if) he is returned to God's holy hill, Jerusalem, a sacrifice of praise will be offered.

It is important to note that the hope is grounded in remembering. The longing of verse one is founded in memory and this becomes specific in verse four where the memory is of processions to the house of God, again Jerusalem, the community en route to worship the Holy One. The memories of God's presence and of community worship give rise to hope even when hope seems illusory.

Thus, Psalm 42–43 highlights the importance of communal worship, both for the present and, in this psalm, also for the future: the memory of the worshipping community is grounds for hope in difficult times, it carries the psalmist when all else fails.

The Structure of Psalm 42–43

Invocation —
O God–Ps 42:1

Lament —
absence–
Ps 42:1–11
(minus the refrain in verses 5 & 11)

Prayer —
for vindication–
Ps 43:1–2

Prayer —
for God's light and truth, presence–
Ps 43:3

Promise —
worship–
Ps 43:4

Refrain —
Ps 42: 5, 11;
Ps 43: 5

Temple Worship

Many psalms were written for use in the Temple and especially during the main pilgrim feasts. In this they are communal. The psalms gave expression to Israel's collective laments and songs of praise and thanks as the community gathered in worship in the Temple in Jerusalem. The psalms seem to be complementary to the sacrificial nature of Temple worship. This liturgical context is not delineated but the books of Kings and especially Chronicles give insights into the musical and sacrificial aspects of worship. The psalms offer glimpses into these liturgical elements.

Music in the Temple

The psalms were chanted and it is in sung form that they come to life. We catch glimpses of the music associated with worship:

> *to declare your steadfast love in the morning,*
> *and your faithfulness by night,*
> *to the music of the lute and the harp,*
> *to the melody of the lyre. Ps 92:2-3*

> *Praise him with trumpet sound;*
> *praise him with lute and harp!*
> *Praise him with tambourine and dance;*
> *praise him with strings and pipe!*
> *Praise him with clanging cymbals;*
> *praise him with loud clashing cymbals! Ps 150:3-5*

> Chant is a simple melody with a varying number of syllables chanted on each note. A simple melody to which the words were fitted. Gregorian chant is perhaps the best-known form of chant and some scholars believe that it is related to the chants used in the second Temple in Jerusalem.

We see the delight associated with the Temple.

- *But I, through the abundance of your steadfast love,
will enter your house,
I will bow down towards your holy temple
in awe of you. Ps 5:7*

- *How lovely is your dwelling place, O LORD of hosts!
My soul longs, indeed it faints
for the courts of the LORD.
Ps 84:1–2*

Sacrifices were offered daily and increased during the feasts and were accompanied by psalms.

- *Now my head is lifted up
above my enemies all around me,
and I will offer in his tent
sacrifices with shouts of joy;
I will sing and make melody to the LORD. Ps 27:6*

- *I will offer to you a thanksgiving sacrifice
and call on the name of the LORD.
I will pay my vows to the LORD
in the presence of all his people,
in the courts of the house of the LORD,
in your midst, O Jerusalem.
Praise the LORD! Ps 116:17–19*

In the Temple there were Levitical singers, as indicated in the superscriptions, and these had a role in terms of Temple music, especially the Asaphites and Korahites. The psalms with Korah in the superscription were most probably the repertoire of the Korahites and so too with the name Asaph.

At times the Psalter has been designated the hymnbook of the Temple. The context of Temple worship was likely the reason for the composition of many psalms but it was not the only place they were prayed. They were prayed by individuals, by communities gathered in times of distress or joy, and as the Synagogues became a recognised part of life for the people of Israel the psalms shifted into Synagogue worship. Later the Jewish-Christians ensured they remained part of the worship of early Christian communities.

Today both Jews and Christians continue to chant these timeless words as they come before God in distress and in thanks and praise.

Temples

The Temple in Jerusalem was the centre for sacrificial worship by the Jewish people. Many psalms were written to be used in the context of Temple worship. The Temple is also mentioned in many Psalms. The first Israelite temple was built by King Solomon, David's son. It was completed around 950 BCE.

This Temple was destroyed by the Babylonian army in 587 BCE. A second Temple was built, in the time of Nehemiah, Zechariah and Haggai around 520 BCE. This second Temple was very significantly enhanced by King Herod the Great, beginning 20 BCE.

It was in this enhanced Temple that Jesus celebrated the Jewish Feasts. This second Temple was destroyed by the Roman army in 70 CE. The loss of the Temple gave rise to Rabbinic Judaism and at the same time the embryonic Christian community developed.

Jerusalem, Zion, God's holy hill, God's dwelling place, God's tent, are some of the many ways of designating the Temple or God's city where the Temple was located.

Left: Herod's Temple from the Dura Europos Synagogue, Syria, 730 CE

Conclusion: Speaking to the Beloved

The Psalter concludes with a marvellous outpouring of praise. This begins with Psalm 146, whose opening verse is: Praise the LORD or in Hebrew Halleluyah. Each of the subsequent psalms begins the same way. The final one, Psalm 150, reaches its crescendo as its last verse invites: Let everything that breathes praise the LORD. We are invited to join with everything that has life in a celebration of the creator of all life.

Thus concludes the Psalter, having taken us on a roller-coaster ride: lifting our hearts and minds to the Beloved and giving expression to the deepest sorrows and pain in human experience, both individual and communal.

Psalm 1 opened the Psalter with an invitation to find happiness through praying and meditating on Torah. I suspect this was understood to include the five books of psalms. Psalm 150 closes the Psalter with an invitation to praise God's mighty deeds and to join in a festival of life, in this way to express happiness achieved.

We humans experience seasons of orientation, disorientation and reorientation. This fluctuation in life is reflected in the Psalter which invites us to allow our changing lives to find a voice in the psalms. The differing genres, especially lament, thanks and praise, provide a means by which we can give full expression to our changing circumstances and those of the world around us.

The history related to the psalms, especially that of King David, reminds us that the psalms sprang from the life and experience of Israel. The psalmists knew the importance of the traditions about the Creator, Zion, the Temple, the land, the king. The history of the Babylonian Exile shaped the theology of the Psalter. The five books of the Psalter remind the readers that the psalms are rooted in the past and yet they show us the way we should to go forward today.

These texts are poetry: they require us to use our experience and imagination in order to engage truly with them. The images and brevity of language allow multiple meanings to emerge. The parallelism and structures ensure we do not miss the point while allowing a range of interpretations. This poetry was chanted and its rhythmic flow reminds us that it is as a community gathered that we sing with one voice.

Jesus knew these prayers and would have prayed them in his family, his synagogues and in the Temple when he went up to Jerusalem for the feasts. The Evangelists used these texts to allow Jesus to give expression to his deepest emotions and on the cross to cry: My God, My God …

A Friendly Guide to the Book of Psalms invites you to become more familiar with this wonderful part of our shared Jewish and Christian holy texts. It invites you to allow the meaning and depth of the psalms to help you deepen your relationship with God. It prompts you to ask more questions and to excavate this marvellous Book of Psalms so as to know yourself and to speak to the Beloved from your heart.

Glossary

Asaph. According to the Book of Chronicles, Asaph was a singer and seer in David's court. In post Exilic times a group of Levitical singers bears his name and ancestry and is portrayed in Chronicles as chief among the Levitical singers in Second Temple times. There are twelve psalms which have in their superscription *l'asaph* (Pss 50, 73-83). These may be their repertoire.

BCE and CE. Before the Common Era and Common Era. It is a recognition that for many people Jesus Christ is not the reference point that he is for Christians. It is an alternative to BC and AD.

Bible, Scripture, Word of God, TaNaK. These are different names for the Bible. The term bible is not specific because when used by members of different traditions it has somewhat different meanings. Catholics include the Old Testament, including the Deutero-canonical books, and the New Testament; Orthodox Christians have the same as Catholics but also include a few more books, the Reform traditions include the New Testament and the Hebrew Old Testament texts while the Jews include only the Hebrew books. Word of God is an expression by believers who understand the Bible as revelation. Scripture is a reference to the written nature of the text, the holy writings. TaNaK is a Jewish reference to the three-fold nature of the Jewish Bible. (T = Torah/Pentateuch, N = Neviim/Prophets, K = Kituvim/Writings). For Christians, 'Word of God' also refers to Jesus who is the Word made flesh. In this book, it is used as a way of speaking of the Scriptures, the Bible.

Bible Translations. The New Revised Standard Version (NRSV) is used in the Friendly Guides. It tries to stay as close to the Hebrew text as possible while making sense to English speakers. Other recommended translations are: RSV, NEB, JPS, NJB. Some translations are literal and can be less clear in terms of meaning. Some translations are very free in attempting to translate into modern English but stray from the original text.

Eschatological. This pertains to a study of last things. It looks towards a future time, the end time. It is linked with a view of history which understands that God has a plan and will bring it and this world to completion. Judgement and death are associated with eschatological texts.

Followers of the Way. The early Christians were known by this name.

Genre. A way of categorising similar pieces of music or literature. In the psalms the most common genres are: lament, hymn, thanksgiving. There are also Wisdom psalms, Torah psalms, Zion psalms, Royal psalms and Liturgies.

Jebusites. This was a Canaanite group which lived in Jerusalem before King David captured the city and made it his capital. This happened around 1000 BCE.

Korah, Korahites. This is another group of Levitical singers. Pss 42-49, 84-5, 88-89 have in their superscription *'of the sons of Korah'* or *'of the Korahites'*. Their ancestor, Korah, was a problematic figure yet his descendants retained their role in the liturgy of the Second Temple.

Levitical Singers. A group with liturgical responsibilities within the temple complex. It seems they had a role in singing but not in the sacrifices. They were subordinate to the priests. The name is derived from the tribe of Levi.

Maskil. This is from the Hebrew word 'maskil' or maschil', meaning enlightened or wise.

Messiah. This is a Hebrew word which literally means an anointed one, anointed with oil. Usually kings, priests and prophets were anointed. It later became a technical term for a future priest/king. The followers of Jesus used this term to speak of him and in Greek it is translated as Christos.

New Testament. The books included in the NT are agreed by all Christians. However, it is important to note that the term Christian Scriptures is not an equivalent to NT. The Christian Scriptures begin with the Book of Genesis and conclude with the Book of Revelation.

Old Testament, Hebrew Bible, Older Testament, First Testament. These are terms used to designate the books of the Bible which belong to the Jewish community and a variety of Christian communities. The difficulty is that there are different lists of books in the canon of the Bible. The Jewish community and the Reform Christians have the same books in their Hebrew Bible/Old Testament but in a different order. The Roman Catholics have some extra books and the Orthodox Christians have even more books in their Bible. For Roman Catholics and Orthodox Christians, the term Hebrew Bible does not include some of their books, which were extant in Greek rather than Hebrew. The term Old Testament, which was historically used by Christians, has sometimes implied that these books are old and therefore not important. Older Testament retains the same initials and is seen to be more respectful. First Testament is chronological and can be more neutral. Jews usually use the term TaNaK. See **Bible** above.

Parallelism. This is a characteristic of Hebrew poetry. In its simplest form it refers to the way one verse seems to repeat itself. The first half of the verse is paralleled by the second half of the verse. The subject, verb and object all have a parallel in the second half of the verse. When this is attended to it becomes clear that the two halves of the verse interplay to expand the meaning.

Patristic interpretations. A name referring to the early Christian scholars (Fathers of the Church) who interpreted the Scriptures. Approximately: 100 CE – 500 CE.

Psalm. The word comes from Greek *psalmos*. It refers to a song accompanied by a stringed instrument. This name reminds us that the psalms were chanted and of their worship context. The closest Hebrew equivalent is *mizmor* but this is not the word by which Jews name the Book of Psalms. Jews call the book *Tehillim*, or praises.

Synagogue. The Temple in Jerusalem was the official place of sacrificial worship. However, there slowly arose another place of non-sacrificial worship. This may have begun as gatherings in homes. Eventually synagogues were purpose-built. The local community gathered for readings and prayers. Since the destruction of the Second Temple in 70 CE the synagogue has been the place for the Jewish community to gather for worship. It must be remembered that the Jewish home is a very important place for prayer and for engaging the tradition in the context of family. The earliest mention of a synagogue is in the 3rd century BCE. The Gospels mention Jesus in the synagogue in Nazareth and in Capernaum.

Temple. There were attempts to build temples in the Northern Kingdom but these did not last and eventually the one temple in Jerusalem was both the actual and theological focus. The First Temple of Jerusalem, built in the time of King Solomon, was destroyed by the Babylonians in 587 BCE. The Second Temple was built when some of the community returned to Jerusalem, after the defeat of the Babylonians. This Second Temple is usually dated 515 BCE. It was destroyed by the Romans in 70 CE.

Further Reading

*Bergant, Diane *Psalms 1-72* and *Psalms 73-150*. Collegeville PA: Liturgical Press, 2013

Brown, William P. *Seeing the Psalms: A Theology of Metaphor*. Louisville KY: Westminster John Knox Press, 2012

Brown, W P (ed) *The Oxford Handbook of the Psalms*. Oxford: OUP, 2014.

*Brueggemann, Walter *Spirituality of The Psalms*. Minneapolis MN: Fortress Press, 2002

*Brueggemann, Walter *The Message of the Psalms*. Minneapolis MN: Augsburg, 1984. (2nd ed 2003)

Brueggemann, W. & W. Bellinger *Psalms* NCBC. Cambridge: University Press, 2014

*Chatham, James *Psalm Conversations*. Collegeville MN: Liturgical Press, 2018

deClaisse-Walford, N.L. *Introduction to the Psalms: A Song from Ancient Israel*. St Louis MO: Chalice Press, 2004.

deClaisse-Walford, N, R. Jacobson & B. Tanner *The Book of Psalms*. NICOT. Grand Rapids MI: Eerdmans, 2014

Estes, Daniel *Handbook on the Wisdom Books and Psalms* Grand Rapids MI: Baker Academic Press, 2010

Jacobson, Rolf (ed) *Soundings in the Theology of Psalms: Perspectives and Methods in Contemporary Scholarship* Minneapolis: Fortress Press, 2011.

Longman, Tremper *Psalms* TOTC Downers Grove IL: Intervarsity Press, 2014

*Magonet, J. *A Rabbi Reads the Psalms*. London: SCM, 1994.

*Nowell, I *Pleading, Cursing, Praising: Conversing with God through the Psalms*. Collegeville, MN: Liturgical Press, 2013.

Tanner, Beth *The Psalms for Today*. Louisville KY: Westminster John Knox Press, 2008

* The books marked with an asterisk are a good place to begin.

My help comes from the LORD, who made heaven and earth.
Ps 121:2

www.ingramcontent.com/pod-product-compliance
Lightning Source LLC
Chambersburg PA
CBHW061059170426
43199CB00025B/2937